Fly-rodding
for Bass

Books by A. D. Livingston

The Sky's the Limit

Poker Strategy and Winning Play

Dealing with Cheats

Fishing for Bass

Advanced Bass Tackle and Boats

Fly-rodding for Bass

Fly-rodding for Bass

by A. D. Livingston

J. B. Lippincott Company
Philadelphia & New York

Grateful acknowledgment is made to the following for the use of material in this book:

Joel Arrington of the Travel and Promotion Division of the State of North Carolina for the photographs on pages 25, 102, 130, and 176.

Field & Stream for the quotation on pages 110–11 from "Basics on Bass Behavior" by Buck Rogers.

The Pennsylvania Fish Commission for the drawing on page 101 from "Identifying the Common Fishes of Pennsylvania" and for the photograph on page 103.

Scientific Anglers/3M for the drawings on pages 35 and 157.

Stone Wall Press, Inc., for the quotation on pages 171–72 from *Fly Casting with Bill Cairns,* © 1974 by Stone Wall Press, Lexington, Massachusetts.

The Tennessee Valley Authority for the photographs on pages 114, 119, and 138.

U.S. Library of Congress Cataloging in Publication Data

Livingston, A   D   birth date
    Fly-rodding for bass.

    Includes index.
    1. Black bass fishing.   2. Fly fishing. I. Title.
SH681.L55   799.1'7'58   75–38710
ISBN–0–397–01112–1

for Helen

Preface

WHEN I FIRST WROTE this preface, I rambled on for five or six pages, exploring in my mind the virtues of fishing for bass with a fly rod. Then I decided to come right to the point: The best reason for using a fly rod is that it will at times catch more bass. That's right. There are times when bugs and flies will outfish hardware and even soft plastic worms. I have proved this, at least to my own satisfaction, on a number of occasions. Why? I believe it is a matter of presenting the lure. Anything cast with spinning or baitcasting gear is likely to splash down in the water. A bug or a fly, though, can be made to roll over and sit down quite gently. This delivery is difficult to match with any other casting gear, and it can be deadly on skittish bass in shallow water.

I might add that in experienced hands the fly rod is capable of pinpoint accuracy, which can be of extreme importance in bass fishing.

In any case, more and more anglers are going after black bass with fly rods. Some of these are experienced bassmen who are adding a fly rod to their several baitcasting and spinning rigs. Others are trout anglers who, finding wild trout fast disappearing from the streams in some areas, decide to go after bass. I hope that the bassman will be pleased, if somewhat surprised, to learn that his fly rod is a real aid to catching fish, not merely something light and sporting. And I trust that the trout angler who is disgruntled with put-and-take hatchery fish will find the black bass—one of the most intelligent of the fresh-water game fish—to be a worthy opponent and one that is now plentiful North, South, East, and West.

Good fishing. Keep your bug sharp and your backcast high.

A. D. LIVINGSTON

Contents

Part One

Selecting Tackle and Gear

FLY-FISHING IS NEITHER difficult to learn nor strenuous to perform if the angler has the right gear. But casting a large, heavy, wind-resistant bug with a rod and line that were designed for tiny dry flies is well nigh impossible. Neither impeccable casting form nor sheer muscle power will get a 2/0 bug out 50 feet unless rod, line, and leader are at least adequate for the job. The first step toward easy bass bugging is to balance your tackle, and I hope that the following chapters will be helpful.

1
Rods

ONCE I KNEW a veteran bass angler in Florida who enjoyed a few citrus trees in his backyard. One night, some years ago, he was lazing before his TV set when a commercial started advertising a new imitation fruit drink. Upon hearing that the newfangled stuff contained more vitamin C than orange juice, he jumped up and shook his fist. "That's a damned lie!" he said. "I've been drinking orange juice all my life." Well, the fact that he had been drinking orange juice all his life has no bearing on the vitamin C content of imitation drinks. I suspect that many anglers apply the same sort of logic, or lack of it, to their fishing rods. Because an old favorite fits the hand comfortably and has turned many a fish doesn't necessarily make it superior to a newer rod.

Other anglers are outright suckers for anything that's new. If one of these tackle freaks had been watching the TV commercial, he would have jumped up and sped off to the nearest grocery store in search of the new instant nectar, even if he had seven gallons of fresh orange juice in the refrigerator. If the store happened to be closed, he would arouse the manager in the middle of the night. If

he couldn't find any of the new stuff in local stores, he would tele-
phone the manufacturer long distance to place a rush order for two
dozen cases, C.O.D. He would then lie awake at night while waiting
for the stuff to arrive, his mouth juicy, his taste buds tangy, his vim
rising just at the thought of all that vitamin C.

Nothing that I say here will be likely to change anglers of either
extreme. But I do believe that the guy who has been using the same
old rod for 20 years would improve his casting and enjoy it more if
he would try a carefully selected modern stick. I also believe that the
guy who thinks that a new space-age wand is going to land a record
bass for him would probably catch more fish by getting on the lake
instead of swishing rods around in tackle shops.

In any case, fly rods have been greatly improved in recent years,
and the modern angler has a wide range of quality rods from which
to choose. Although fiberglass currently dominates the market, bamboo is still prized by some anglers, and high-modulus graphite is coming on strong. Each of these materials has advantages and disadvantages, as discussed below:

Bamboo. Although the typical bamboo rod is a bit heavier than
a comparable fiberglass stick, the material has some highly desirable
casting qualities. Bamboo is a little stiffer than fiberglass, but it loads
well and seems somehow to help the angler with the cast more than
fiberglass does. Perhaps its distinguishing characteristic is that it
doesn't vibrate as much as fiberglass. It dampens quicker and casts
a straighter line.

A big disadvantage is that top-quality raw materials are in short
supply and that building a split-bamboo rod requires a lot of crafts-
manship. The result is that top-notch bamboo rods are quite expensive, usually over $100. Another disadvantage is that bamboo rods
require careful handling and constant attention if they are to last
very long. If they are stored improperly, they may "set" or warp.
Some will rot if moisture seeps under the finish, so that they must be
inspected frequently for chipped spots; but modern fabrication techniques, such as waterproofing the blank throughout by impregnating
it with resin, have gone a long way toward overcoming this problem.

Still, I can't recommend bamboo for bass fishing. In my opinion, it
is more suited for short rods designed to cast light lines and delicate
flies. My objection to bamboo is based not on casting performance
but on practical fishing. Bass anglers accustomed to setting hooks with
stiff worm rods are likely either to break the tip of a bamboo rod or

be far too conscious of what they are fishing with. In most cases, a bassman needs a rod tough enough to horse lunkers out of thick lily pads or treetops. It is the habits of the black bass, not its size, that almost force the angler to use a comparatively heavy leader and a rather stout rod. Such a rod made from bamboo would be a little heavy for making repeated casts all day.

Anyhow, it's my opinion that bamboo rods just aren't practical for general bass fishing, although I concede that the experienced fly-rodder can certainly use bamboo sticks with excellent results.

Fiberglass. From a casting standpoint, fiberglass may not be the ideal stuff from which to make rod blanks, but it does make a very good fishing stick. It's tough. It's light. It doesn't take a set as readily

The author makes a roll cast with an inexpensive fiberglass rod. Note the irregular line near the rod tip. This is caused by vibration, one of the biggest problems with fiberglass fly rods.

as bamboo. It doesn't rot, and, in general, it can be kicked around more than bamboo. There is no shortage of the material, and it lends itself well to mass production techniques. What's more, modern manufacturing processes have vastly improved fiberglass rods since they were introduced—shortly after World War II. And improvements continue. Fiberglass rods currently dominate the market, and this itself is an advantage simply because a wide choice of blanks is available at reasonable prices.

There are, of course, some rather expensive fiberglass rods on the market. The difference between an expensive rod and an inexpensive one is often not merely the quality of the blank. It's the fittings and workmanship required to finish off the rod. Indeed, both an expensive and an inexpensive rod might well be made from identical off-the-shelf blanks.

The biggest problem with fiberglass, at least from the viewpoint of casting, is that it vibrates more than either bamboo or graphite. A vibrating tip can cause waves in the fly line, as well as causing rod slap when one is shooting line. But this vibration isn't too much of a problem in bass fishing at normal casting distances, and the vibration in fiberglass rods certainly isn't as severe as it was in the old steel rods.

Everything considered, a good fiberglass rod is by far the best buy for anyone with budget limitations.

Graphite. A material developed in aerospace research, high-modulus graphite is tough and stiff and light. A rod blank made of graphite fibers is about 25 percent lighter than a comparable fiberglass blank and some 40 percent lighter than a comparable bamboo blank. But these figures are only for the blanks; the handles and fittings would weigh about the same, so that the weights of finished rods wouldn't make graphite look quite so good. On the other hand, I for one appreciate even an ounce of savings in weight, especially when I am making repeated casts with a heavy fly line and bass bugs.

Another point is that a typical graphite rod is much smaller in diameter than either a fiberglass or a bamboo rod; this reduces wind resistance, which might be more important than a savings in weight. As a casting stick, a typical graphite rod holds a tighter loop and throws a fast, almost wave-free line. A faster line speed permits more distance, if the angler has the mechanics down pat.

The big disadvantage of graphite rods is that they cost too much. The first ones, made by Fenwick, retailed at about $200. But some retailers discounted them considerably, and, now that other firms are marketing graphite rods, the prices are dropping somewhat. I've seen an 8-foot rod priced at less than $100. My only fear now is that too many firms have jumped in too quickly, concentrating on getting out a graphite blank instead of thoroughly researching the material's potential. I talked recently to the president of a large rod company, and, if I understood him correctly, he feels that thus far the manufacturers have been trying to design around the properties of high-modulus graphite instead of making use of these properties. He is, of course, interested in graphite and is working with it, but so far his firm hasn't rushed into production.

Although a good deal has already been written about high-modulus graphite, I rather doubt that anybody fully understands the stuff and its application to fishing rods. As I said in my book *Advanced Bass Tackle and Boats,* I think it's a whole new ball game not only for anglers but also for rod designers and theorists. I believe that the material will require new rod standards and specifications. For one thing, I am puzzled because the material is very stiff, yet seems to load well. And graphite seems to handle a wider range of line weights. I personally feel that the material's greatest potential is in very long fly rods, from 10 to 12 feet, simply because of its light weight and the reduced wind resistance of the finished rod.

I like the graphite rods I have used, but I certainly can't vouch for every model that's hitting the market. And just because I like a certain rod doesn't mean that another angler will. My advice is that the bassman should certainly try graphite if he has the money to spare. Over the long run, graphite might turn out to be the best investment one can make in a good rod. Both fiberglass and bamboo will in time more or less wear out. Flexing will eventually change the stiffness of the fibers, and the rod will become more limber. Although the rod will probably still be strong enough, its casting properties will be altered. And this is not necessarily a function of time; it depends entirely on the number of casts made. Trout anglers who seldom cast until they see a rise, or a saltwater angler who stalks bonefish, might use a good rod for many, many years. A bassman, on the other hand, knows that he will increase his chances by keeping his bug in the water; armed with baitcasting rigs, some of the bass pros make as many as 10 casts per minute, all day long. Anyhow, high-modulus graphite fibers do not suffer any apparent materials fatigue after repeated flexing. It's something to think about. On the other

Here's a nice bass the author caught on a 1¾-ounce graphite rod.

hand, graphite rods are apparently more likely to break once they have been nicked or chipped, and questions have been raised about whether the graphite fibers will in time separate from the resin.

Note that it is easy to make a lousy fly rod from the very best and most expensive raw materials. It's also easy to ruin even the best blank by altering it slightly or by putting the hardware on incorrectly. I feel, therefore, that design and workmanship are more important than materials. Whether you choose a bamboo, fiberglass, or graphite rod, it must be properly designed, unerringly manufactured, and painstakingly fitted out before it will give good service for a long time.

A rod blank's performance will depend largely on length, weight, and action.

Action. Rod blanks are classified as slow, medium, fast, and extra-fast, depending on how they bend under a load. Although many anglers (especially hardware slingers) think of rod action in terms of taper, the slow-medium-fast classification is more helpful in understanding the mechanics of casting. It's a matter of time and timing. Unless one is using a rigid stick, a rod blank bends during a cast. If it bends from tip to butt, it's slow and takes longer to recoil. If it bends only in the tip end, it's fast.

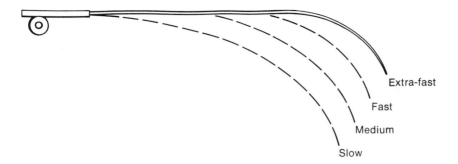

Extra-fast
Fast
Medium
Slow

I prefer a slow rod for bass fishing because it works better for me, and because it isn't as tiring as a fast rod. A slow, full-flex rod can be almost an extension of the casting arm, permitting a smooth, continuous power stroke. But casting isn't the only consideration. A fast rod with a stiff midsection and butt is better for setting large hooks and is also better for horsing bass out of treetops. A good compromise would be a medium-action rod, whether it be for baitcasting, spinning, or fly-fishing.

One problem is that it is difficult to tell from some manufacturers' literature, or from the description in some mail-order catalogs, exactly which action a rod has. Some outfits don't even mention rod action, as if the fact that they market the stick is all one needs to know. Others specify "bass action," "steelhead action," and so on. Still others use such terms as "power" and "taper." Most manufacturers of quality rods, however, and most mail-order houses will answer your questions about rod actions. In a tackle shop, you may or may not get a correct answer. (I've seen some tackle shops that put open-faced spinning reels on saltwater popping rods!) The best bet, when considering a rod off the rack, is to test the action yourself. Most anglers take a rod off a rack and swish it up and down, but the correct way to study the action is to jam the butt against your belly, hold the handle with both hands, and swish the rod horizontally. Watch how it bends and you can pretty much determine its action. It is sometimes questionable whether a rod is slow or medium, but this method is generally foolproof in detecting the fast, tip-action sticks.

Weight. The weight or "power" of a rod is a separate design variable and should not be confused with action or "taper." The weight of any good rod is matched to the weight it was designed to cast, regardless of whether that weight be plug, live bait, or fly line.

One simply can't cast a heavy weight satisfactorily with a light rod, or a light weight with a heavy rod.

Fortunately, most fly-rod manufacturers now rate their blanks in accordance with the line-weight standards established by the American Fishing Tackle Manufacturers' Association, as will be discussed more fully in Chapter 3. Not all manufacturers mark their rods or rod blanks according to the weight line they are designed to cast, but the practice is becoming more common each year. Virtually all the better mail-order houses list this information in their catalogs.

Although the beginner will do well to match rod and line strictly according to the manufacturer's instructions or recommendations, there is some room for deviation. Most rods will perform pretty well if they are used with a line one size larger or one size smaller than what the rod manufacturer specifies. It's been my experience, however, that rods used for bass fishing work better if they are slightly overloaded than if they are underloaded. For one thing—and this is basic—it takes a heavier line to carry a bass bug. For another, bass anglers frequently make short casts, which are generally a little easier to execute with a slightly overloaded rod.

The best bet, however, is to stick with the rod manufacturer's recommendations until you have good reason to deviate from them.

Length. Within limits, the longer the rod the greater the distance it will cast a fly line. There *are* limits, however, beyond which a rod simply becomes unwieldy. For general bass fishing, an 8½-foot rod of suitable weight and action is about right. An 8-foot rod will do, and so will a 9-footer. But I feel that 9-foot rods designed for salt-water use or for distance casting are on the border line and will overly fatigue the bass angler; although these long, hefty rods might cast bass bugs wondrously for a while, they are simply too heavy to wield all day, cast after cast. There may, however, be an opening here for long, thin, light graphite rods, but at the time of this writing long graphite blanks are hard to come by. I understand that Fenwick has recently introduced a 10½-foot graphite rod designed for steelhead anglers, but so far I haven't been able to lay my hands on one. As applied to bass fishing, the advantage of such a long rod is that it would make the pickup easier, and this can be important when trying to get some bass bugs out of the water. A disadvantage is that such a long rod would, in my opinion, make short, accurate casts more difficult, and, if my experience is typical, the bass angler makes a lot of casts under 30 feet.

On the short side, I wouldn't recommend any stick less than 8 feet long. And limited distance isn't the only reason. It's a matter of timing. Short rods that are stiff enough to handle a bass-bug line require a much faster cast, thereby making the timing more critical. What's more, short, stiff rods are downright dangerous when used to cast heavy bugs. I tried to fish with a stiff 7-foot rod that was designed to take a No. 8 line, but I soon put the thing up because I hadn't brought any ear muffs or helmet along. Anyhow, one problem with short rods and heavy bugs is that the pickup is difficult, which in turn gets the backcast off to a bad start.

If I had to make recommendations based on what I've already said, I would come up with an 8½-foot, 8-weight, medium- or slow-action fly rod. It wouldn't be ideal for every aspect of bass fishing, but it would do just about anything, anytime, anywhere. Indeed, it might even be better to stick with such a basic rod and learn how to use it well instead of jumping from one length and action to another. But, in all honesty, I wouldn't want to do all my fishing with one rod!

In any case, here are a few additional points to consider when selecting and using a fly rod:

Guides and tips. In normal fly-fishing, the rod guides and tips are not subjected to as much wear and friction as they are in baitcasting and spinning with artificial lures. The reason is that usually the fly line is not shot through and pulled back over the guides on every cast. After working out some line, the fly fisherman might make any number of casts without stripping in or shooting out more than a few feet of line. Also, fly-rod lures are generally fished slower than hardware and are not usually retrieved all the way to the rod tip. Even so, the guides and tip on a fly rod should be inspected from time to time. A good fly line is expensive, and there's no point in wearing it out with abrasive guides and tip.

Traditionally, fly rods are fitted with snake guides, except for a stripping guide or two on the butt end. Snake guides are made from wire in the shape of a spiral but without forming a closed loop. The ends are flattened so that the rod winding thread can bind them to the blank tightly. The tip is usually made from a rather pear-shaped loop of wire with the ends soldered into a metal tube, which in turn fits over the end of the rod blank. A big advantage of wire guides and tips is that they are light.

Stripping guides have a metal frame and are fitted with a hard ring, very much like guides on the better baitcasting rods. I personally prefer aluminum oxide or "ceramic" rings to metal ones, but either tungsten carbide or hard stainless steel rings are usually used. Tungsten carbide rings are also used in the tips of the heavier fly rods, but the material is too heavy for light blanks. Again, I prefer aluminum oxide rings.

Some fly rods designed for distance shooting are now being fitted with the wire Foulproof guides, and some anglers are going to the light Fuji aluminum oxide ring guides. There is no doubt that either type of ring guide lets the line shoot through with less friction, thereby permitting more distance. These guide rings also help keep the line away from the blank, which reduces rod slap. If you do a lot of distance casting, then you certainly should consider light ring guides. But remember that you can alter the action of a rod by tampering even slightly with the weight or the spacing of the guides.

Grips. Most fly-rod grips are made by slipping cork rings over the rod blank, setting them with glue, and then shaping them. Half a dozen shapes have been more or less standardized, but cigar-shaped grips are probably more common than all the rest put together. Any grip that is comfortable throughout the cast is satisfactory, and my only comment along this line is that some grips on very light fly rods are too small in diameter, at least for me.

Most of the better off-the-shelf fly rods are available only in a standard grip. If you're fussy about grips and want something especially for your hand, the best bet is to talk to a rod maker. Or do it yourself. Some of the firms listed in the Appendix market cork rings, reel seats, and other rod-making tools and materials.

Reel seats. Most of the inexpensive or moderately priced fly rods are fitted with fixed reel seats made from anodized aluminum alloy, or some such light metal. Usually, a hood (or cup) is fixed to the end of the rod and is part of the butt cap. A similar hood slides up and down a barrel (which is threaded on one end) and can be tightened onto the forward reel foot by knurled rings. Double-locking seats have two knurled rings. Some of the more expensive rods, especially bamboo, have a hardwood barrel with silver-nickel screw mechanisms on the forward end.

Very light rods, and a few heavier sticks, often have the entire reel seat made of cork, and the reel is held in place by two metal friction rings, without any sort of screw mechanism. I own a 1¾-ounce rod that is fitted with sliding rings, and they work very well. Frankly, I would just as soon have simple rings on all my fly rods. And on spinning rods.

Ferrules. In order to avoid such terms as "ferruleless ferrules," I'll hereby define a fishing rod ferrule as any plug-and-socket arrangement that joins two sections of a rod to each other.

I prefer solid blanks for baitcasting and spinning rods, but fly rods almost have to break apart for the convenience of toting them around. But two-piece fly rods are better than three-piece. The fewer the ferrules, the more continuous and uniform the blank.

Most of the better fiberglass rods made these days have glass-to-glass ferrules. And graphite rods have graphite-to-graphite. Some of the better bamboo rods have 18 percent nickel-silver ferrules, and a lot of custom-made rods, as well as production models, are fitted with new anodized aluminum ferrules with replaceable rubber O-rings on the plug. Arguments could be made for and against any of the better quality ferrules. Glass-to-glass ferrules, or graphite-to-graphite, are generally trouble-free and don't stick together as often as metal ferrules; if they are damaged, however, or if they wear too much, the rod owner has serious problems. Metal ferrules can be replaced easily, but they are prone to bind and can be a pain in the neck. Proper care and lubrication can save the angler some time in the long run.

From a casting viewpoint, I prefer glass-to-glass or graphite-to-graphite ferrules on either fiberglass or graphite rods, simply because they bend with the rod more than metal ferrules do. But the difference is probably very slight, and the actual effect on casting may be mostly imaginary. If I made my own rods from uncut blanks, I'd certainly go with the anodized aluminum ferrules with the replaceable O-rings.

2

Fly Reels

MORE THAN ONCE it has been said that all the reel does in fly-fishing is store the line. I've said it myself. Although the reel can be used to take in slack line and to help do battle with a large fish, the spool doesn't pay out line during the cast; and this lack of function tends to belittle the importance of good reel design. It's true that the basic purpose of the fly reel *is* to store the line, but how it stores the line can either facilitate or foil easy casting—especially when the angler is shooting for distance.

The ideal fly reel has a narrow span (about 1 inch) and a large-diameter spool (from 3 to 4 inches, depending on the size of the fly line and the amount of the backing line to be used on the reel). Such a spool has two definite advantages. First, the large diameter doesn't cause too much "coil set" in the fly line. Coiled and kinky line makes shooting difficult, and, in extreme cases, can tangle a line so badly that the angler may break off a large fish because a knotted line jammed at one of the rod guides. Second, a large, full spool makes for a fast retrieve, which can be helpful in taking up slack line either when working a bass bug or when a hooked fish runs toward the angler. Another advantage of the design is that the large-diameter spools can be ventilated with holes in the sides and the narrow span permits air to circulate through the spooled line.

Here are some additional considerations:

1. A good drag system is highly desirable on any reel, and especially on a fly reel used together with a light leader tippet.

2. Because a fly line is only 30 or 35 yards long, the reel should have the capacity for backing line. Thinking only in terms of weight, many anglers err by getting a reel that is too small. I've made that mistake myself, and once I ordered an automatic reel that wouldn't even hold all the fly line I intended to use, much less 100 yards of backing line.

3. A reel with interchangeable spools will enable the angler to switch quickly from one fly line to another. Some anglers use three or even four spools.

This nice stringer of bass was taken in North Carolina.

4. A click ratchet is needed to prevent the spool from overturning and fouling the line.

The angler should keep the preceding points in mind when choosing from the three basic types of fly reel:

Single-action reels. If I had to choose one reel for all my fly-fishing, I would quickly take a good single-action model with a large-diameter spool. These reels are mechanically simple, light in weight, and generally trouble-free. The term "single action" refers to a reel with a 1-to-1 retrieve ratio; the angler turns the reel spool directly, without a gear train. The only disadvantage of single-action reels is that taking up slack line is slow when compared with multiplying or automatic fly reels. Although the faster reels may be desirable at times, the single-action is usually quite adequate for bass fishing and for most other forms of fly-fishing, considering the fact that the relatively large spool hauls in lots of line per turn. A reel with a 4-inch diameter, for example, hauls in about a foot of line per revolution when the spool is filled to capacity.

Single-action fly reel.

The cheaper single-action reels have no drag system, except possibly for a click ratchet. The better models have either an internal drag that works on some sort of adjustable brake system or a manual "rim" drag. I prefer the rim drag, in which all or part of the outer side of the revolving spool is accessible. When a fish is taking out line, the angler cups the rim in his hand and adjusts the pressure on the spool. Thus, the experienced angler can instantly increase or decrease the drag. The big drawback to the rim drag is that it somewhat complicates reel design and construction, and is therefore usually available only on expensive reels.

Most of the better fly reels have interchangeable spools. This highly desirable feature is well suited to single-action reels. Some of the more expensive reels have a one-sided frame. This design permits the interchangeable spools to snap on and off in a second, and, of course, such a spool is ideal for rim braking. But these reels have to be made to precise tolerances if they are to give good service for a long time. Usually, the aluminum spool and the frame are machined from aluminum bar stock so that each is one piece, without screws or rivets.

On some less expensive reels, the spool fits inside a cage-type frame, a design that complicates rim braking. Some of these cage reels, however, do have a good internal, adjustable drag system, as well as interchangeable spools.

Multiplying reels. A single-action reel doesn't have a true handle. Instead, it has a knob mounted near the outer edge of the revolving spool. A multiplying reel does have a true handle, fitted into the center of the spool. The handle is attached to a gear train, which usually turns the spool at a ratio of about 3 to 1.

The big advantage of a multiplying reel is that it takes up slack line faster than a single-action reel—a feature that can be quite helpful, and can save the day, when a fast fish runs toward the angler. The disadvantage of multiplying reels is that they are heavier than single-action reels. They are also more complicated and are therefore more likely to cause mechanical problems. Good ones, however, are quite dependable.

The relatively complicated design of the multiplying reel doesn't lend itself readily to rim braking, so that most of the better multipliers have adjustable internal drag systems. But rim-braked multipliers are possible. The Orvis Magnalite, for example, has an adjustable internal drag system as well as an overlapping spool rim.

Personally, I don't think that multiplying reels are necessary for most bass fishing, and, frankly, I prefer the simplicity of single-action reels. But any angler should certainly consider a multiplier if he plans to use his bass rig for bigger, faster game.

Automatic reels. In the late 1800s, Herman W. Martin, founder of the Martin Reel Company, lost a prize fish because his fly line tangled in the bottom of his boat. He subsequently invented an automatic fly reel that would pick up excess or slack line. However ingenious for the times, the first automatics were crude-looking contraptions as compared with today's streamlined models.

Automatic fly reels work on a loaded-spring principle. When line is stripped off the reel, the spool revolves and tightens a spring. When the retrieve trigger is depressed with the pinkie of the rod hand, the spring tension is released. The spring then turns the spool, zipping in the line. The better reels have a "free-stripping" feature, which allows fly line and backing line to be paid out without overloading the spring. Some automatics also have a spring-tensioning device so that the spring can be loaded without stripping off line, and some models have a release so that the spring won't have to be stored under tension.

The big advantage of automatics is that they can quickly take in excess line, thereby getting it out of the way. This prevents tangled lines, and it also helps keep line out from under the angler's feet. (Standing on a fly line, especially in a boat or on a rocky bank, is a major source of line wear and cracked coating!) In addition, the quick pickup can at times be very helpful in taking in slack when a fish runs toward the angler.

There are, however, several disadvantages to automatic fly reels:

1. Automatics are generally a good deal heavier than manual fly reels. Consequently, they are usually unsuited for use on ultralight rods. Weight as such, however, is not usually a severe problem with fly rods heavy enough to cast large bass bugs. In fact, a relatively heavy reel is usually required to balance most bass sticks.

2. Automatics do not have the line capacity of the larger manual reels of the same weight. This limited line capacity is not as critical in bass angling as in saltwater fishing, but I personally like to have a lot of backing line available just in case I need it. In other words, if I am going to be using a heavy reel, I prefer to have the weight in backing line instead of in steel springs and related mechanisms.

3. Typically, the spool on an automatic reel has a smaller diameter

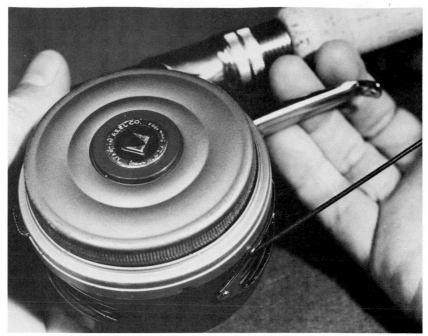

Automatic fly reel.

than a spool on a manual reel of comparable weight. Consequently, line coil is more of a problem with automatics.

4. Because of its mechanical complexity, it is more difficult to design an automatic reel with interchangeable spools. Although some automatics do feature interchangeable spools, the change-out is not as quick as on single-action reels.

5. Automatics are more apt to develop mechanical problems.

6. Lacking handles or manual cranks, automatic reels can't be used for playing down large fish.

7. Automatics are not desirable for use in salt water because of corrosion in the spring mechanisms.

8. While spooled with line, automatics are more difficult to ventilate properly than single-action reels.

In my opinion, the disadvantages of automatics outweigh the advantages of fast line pickup, but I own an automatic and use it from time to time. An automatic comes in handy for night fishing, when tangled lines are more likely to occur, especially if the angler is using a foot-controlled electric motor. I must point out that I also use an

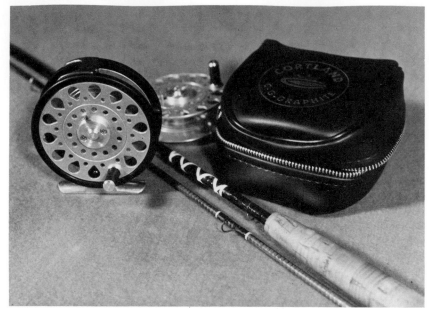

Most of the better reels on the market are made from machined aluminum, but other materials are beginning to appear. The little reel shown here is made by Cortland and some of its parts are graphite. It is 30 percent lighter than comparable aluminum reels.

automatic occasionally to achieve a fast, steady retrieve—but this is highly unconventional!

The price of fly reels varies drastically, from a few dollars to well over a hundred. My first reel, if I remember correctly, cost only $1.98 some years back. It has served me well, and I still use it occasionally —even on a $100 rod! I do, however, prefer to have a more sophisticated reel, especially when I'm in lunker-bass country or when I am bass bugging in waters where larger game fish may hit. When bass fishing in brackish water, for example, one might tie into a large snook or tarpon. I've even caught alligator gar on hair mice when fishing for bass.

I suspect, though, that I more or less insist on having an expensive fly reel not so much from utility but because I enjoy precision gear. The plain truth is that almost any fly reel with a sufficiently large spool will do for bass fishing. So, anglers who are planning to buy a new fly-rodding outfit on a budget can skimp on the reel in order to invest in a good rod. And a top-quality line.

3

Lines, Leaders, and Knots

CHOICE OF LINE is important in all types of fly-rodding, and especially when the angler is casting, or trying to cast, heavy, wind-resistant lures. I don't intend to argue here whether the line is more important than the rod, but if you're going to mismatch your gear it's better to err with a heavy line on a light rod than with a light line on a heavy rod. Being accustomed to baitcasting and spinning gear, more than one bass angler has bought an adequate rod and a line too light for bass bugging. Of course, they fail to realize that in fly-fishing they are casting the line and it pulls the lure behind it up until the turnover, whereas in baitcasting and spinning they cast the lure and it pulls the line. The heavier the plug, the heavier the line it will pull; the heavier the fly line, the heavier the bug it will pull. In baitcasting or spinning, the rod is matched to the weight of the lure; in fly-fishing, the rod is matched to the weight of the line, which in turn is (or should be) selected on the basis of the fly or bug one intends to cast.

In short, it isn't too uncommon for a bassman to purchase the wrong fly line, and to conclude, after a bout or two on the lake, that fly-fishing is a difficult thing. Moreover, bassmen are likely to be taken aback by the price of a top-notch fly line, which may cost $25 or more. Why so much for only 30 yards of line when a spinning reel or baitcasting reel can be spooled with 100 yards of line at a much lower cost? The reason is that a fly line consists of an outer coating over a central core, and the more expensive lines are tapered in one way or another. Such a line is more difficult to manufacture, as compared to monofilament and braided lines of uniform diameter and materials. In spite of the high initial cost, however, a good fly line is actually cheaper over the long run than line used with either spinning or baitcasting gear. With proper care, a good fly line can be used for many years, whereas monofilament and braided lines should be replaced often—sometimes after a single day's fishing. So, buy a good fly line and take care of it.

The first fly lines were made of braided horsehair. Silk was a great improvement, but today such synthetic materials as nylon and dacron pretty much dominate the market. These excellent modern lines re-

Fly lines have been vastly improved in recent years, and the modern angler has a wide selection from which to choose.

quire little care, whereas older lines had to be dressed frequently and thoroughly dried out after each fishing trip. Fly fishermen never had it so good!

Modern fly lines are usually classified according to their density, taper, and weight (or size).

Density. Some fly lines float; others sink. Some are even designed to float *or* sink, depending on whether or not they are treated with line dressing. And some sinking lines sink faster than others. A few lines even have floating midsections and sinking tips.

But most fly-fishing for bass, as well as for other fish, is done with a floating line even when the angler intends to fish a few feet down. The plain truth is that floating lines cast better, or easier, than sinking lines simply because they are easier to pick up from the water. And the higher a line floats, the better I like it. Some of the new foamy lines, such as Scientific Anglers' Air Cel or Cortland's Micro-Foam, are inherently quite buoyant and float beautifully.

A number of manufacturers market small tins of paste for dressing a floating line. Most of it is good stuff, but many anglers tend to use far too much of it in an effort to keep their line afloat when what they really need to do is clean their line thoroughly. In time, enough film and dirt can build up to sink even the most buoyant line. I use mild soap and warm water to remove dirt and film. After my line is cleaned and dried, I apply a sparse coat of dressing. A good dressing not only conditions a line but also lubricates it so that it will shoot smoothly through the rod guides.

If the angler intends to fish deeper than about 5 feet, a sinking line is called for. One *could* fish on down with, say, a 10-foot leader on a floating line, but quite a belly would develop in the line and leader as the lure sank. This belly would make it difficult to detect a pickup and would also make it more difficult to set the hook. Moreover, the lure would go down very slowly unless it were weighted.

Personally, I prefer a sinking tip or a slow-sinking line when I want to fish from 5 to 10 feet down. For deeper fishing, a fast-sinking line works best. The truth is that deep fishing is rather difficult with a fly rod, but it can be done and will be discussed in more detail in Chapter 7.

I have little use for a so-called intermediate line that floats or sinks, but it may be a good choice for budget-minded anglers who want to fish both shallow and deep with the same line. But I think that the best bet is to have two lines and a reel with interchangeable spools. Besides, intermediate lines are not widely available at the usual tackle outlets.

In most cases, the beginner can get by nicely for a while with only a floating line. My best advice is to get a good one and keep it clean. There's nothing more irritating in all types of angling than a floating fly line that sinks.

Taper. I use the term "taper" here only because it is so well established. The bass angler, however, will do well to think in terms of how the weight is distributed along the line instead of how the diameter changes from one point to another. The beginner should be warned that what is usually called a tapered line is unsuited to casting large bass bugs simply because the weight is not properly distributed along the line, although the ideal bassing line *is* tapered. This confusion arises because a tapered line designed to cast tiny dry flies is called a tapered line, whereas a tapered line designed to cast bass bugs and other heavy lures is called a weight-forward line. Here are the four kinds of fly line as determined by weight distribution and taper:

Level lines. The simplest fly line, and the least expensive to manufacture, the level line has a uniform diameter from one end to the other. In other words, such a line has no taper and the weight is evenly distributed. Generally, a level line costs only about 25 percent of the price of a tapered line made of the same material. This wide price gap is simply a matter of manufacturing difficulty. Because they are economical, level lines are commonly used for bass, bluegills, and other fish. And they work satisfactorily provided that they are matched to the rod and the lure. Long casts can be made with level lines *if* the lure is light and not too wind resistant; heavy or highly wind-resistant lures, however, are best cast with a more expensive line, especially if the angler wants good distance.

Tapered lines. A tapered line has a heavy belly that tapers down to a light tip. A *double-tapered* line (as shown in the diagram on the opposite page) is tapered on both ends; consequently, the leader can be attached to either end. The reason for a double taper is that once one end of the line shows signs of wear it can be reversed and the other end will be as good as new. Sounds good, but if a line stays on a spool long, the end attached to the arbor (or to the backing line) will tend to coil excessively.

Anyhow, the purpose of a tapered line is to deliver a small fly

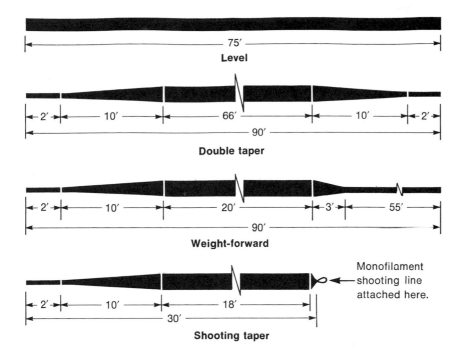

Level

Double taper

Weight-forward

Shooting taper

Monofilament shooting line attached here.

with delicacy and finesse. It is simply not designed to cast bass bugs and large saltwater streamers.

Weight-forward lines. This type has a big, forward belly tapering to a small diameter on the leader end and tapering back to a small rear end. (How the configuration of a weight-forward line differs from a tapered line should be made clear by the accompanying illustration.) The weight-forward line is designed for distance casting with heavy lures. It is ideal for bass fishing. A number of firms market weight-forward lines, and some are called *bass bug taper* or *saltwater taper.* There is some variation, but any good weight-forward line handles bugs satisfactorily *if* the line is matched to the rod and *if* the bug isn't exorbitant in size. If you want to cast large bugs for any distance, try a saltwater taper.

Shooting head. Designed for distance casting, this line is, in essence, a weight-forward line cut in half and attached to a smaller-diameter shooting line. A good shooting head can be made by attaching a shooting line to the first 30 feet of a weight-forward line of suitable weight. Some shooting heads are made with a special shooting line attached (without knots) and some are made with a built-in loop for tying on the shooting line. The shooting line itself can be monofilament (usually about 20-pound) or a floating braided line.

A shooting taper may save the day when long casts are required, as when one is stalking bass in clear, shallow water, or when jump fishing for schooling bass. Normally, however, a shooting head isn't required in bass angling. In any case, a shooting head is of no advantage unless the angler is experienced in fly casting and knows how to handle the coiled shooting line properly.

Bass anglers who want to try deep-structure fishing with a fly rod should know that fast-sinking lead-core shooting heads are available. They can also be made from lead-core trolling line.

Weight. The most basic consideration in the choice of a fly line isn't really whether it floats or sinks, or whether it's tapered or level. It's a matter of weight. If a fly line isn't heavy enough, it simply won't carry a bass bug. If the line is heavier than necessary, it will somewhat overload the rod and tire the angler.

The following table is based on a classification system worked out by the American Fishing Tackle Manufacturers' Association:

Line Number	Weight (in grains)	Tolerance Range
3	100	94–106
4	120	114–126
5	140	134–146
6	160	152–168
7	185	177–193
8	210	202–218
9	240	230–250
10	280	270–290
11	330	318–342
12	380	368–392

Note that the weight is based on the first 30 feet, so that the tapered end is figured in. The important thing to remember when buying modern gear is not the weight in grains but the assigned number. A rod manufacturer, for example, will specify a No. 6 line for a particular rod and a No. 9 for another. The manufacturer's recommendation will usually be about right, but some leeway is possible, depending in part on the particular angler.

The classification of fly lines according to density, taper, and weight (or size) is not really difficult, as I hope I have made clear in the discussions above. Even after an angler understands the classification system, he might be stumped when he first sees all the pertinent information jammed together in code form in a catalog or on a line's label. I know one seasoned bass fly-rodder who has never understood the business, can't read a label, and relies on his salesman to guide him in the selection of a line. Fortunately, he has a salesman who knows his stuff. I might add that a good fly-gear salesman is hard to find in most parts of the country.

The code isn't complicated if one understands fly lines and will take a few seconds to puzzle it out. All modern fly lines made in this country (and most that are made abroad and marketed in this country) are coded by taper, weight (size), and type (density), as for example L-9-F. The first part of the code designates the taper (L = level). The middle digit designates the size or weight. The last part designates the type (F = floating). Here's the key:

Taper	Size (or Weight)	Type (Density)
L = level	3 = 100 grains	F = floating
DT = double taper	4 = 120 grains	S = sinking
WF = weight-forward	etc. (See	SM = medium sinking
ST = shooting taper	previous table	SF = fast sinking
	for line numbers,	SXF = extra-fast
	typical weights,	sinking
	and tolerance	FS = sinking tip
	ranges.)	I = intermediate

Thus, a WF-9-F line would be a weight-forward size 9 floating line. This system is now commonly used in this country, and I'm not going to confuse the issue by getting into obsolete codes.

One reason for using a leader is that it is less visible than a heavy fly line. Another reason is that the leader permits the angler to deliver his lure more gently. Both visibility and presentation are important in bass angling, but not usually as critical as in trout angling. Yet the leader design is more important when you are trying to cast heavy bugs than when you are casting dainty dry flies. Visibility aside, the bass angler will do well to consider his leader as a vital link between line and bug. The leader transmits energy from the fly line to the lure, and a leader of inadequate stiffness simply will not work properly. A leader consisting merely of a 9-foot length of

6-pound monofilament, for example, will not turn a bug over; the cast made with such a leader and a heavy bug will be incomplete more often than not, with the bug falling short of the mark amid a coil of leader. A single length of 20-pound monofilament would work better, but it is not normally desirable to have such a heavy tippet because of visibility and because a heavier tippet can kill the action of light lures. The best bet, then, is to use a tapered leader with a heavy butt and a light tippet.

It is possible to purchase ready-made tapered leaders, but in my opinion it's better, and certainly cheaper, to tie your own from monofilament.

For bass fishing, I normally tie a leader about 7 or 8 feet long, or a little shorter than the fly rod I am using. If I want a 7-foot leader tapered for a No. 9 fly line, I'll usually use about 4 feet of 25-pound monofilament, 1½ feet of 17-pound, and 1½ feet of 10-pound tippet. If I want a 6-pound tippet, I merely tie 8 inches or so to the 10-pound. It may be better to step down in 5-pound increments, maybe with 3 feet of 25-pound, 1½ feet of 20, 1½ feet of 15, and 1 foot of 10. But I try to keep my leaders simple in order to reduce the number of knots required.

The main thing about a leader for bass fishing is that the butt must be stiff enough to turn the bug over. *Usually* a 25-pound monofilament is about right for a No. 9 line, but I usually go up to a 30-pound with a No. 10 line and (usually) down to a 20-pound with a No. 8 line. If I seem to be overworking the word "usually," and seem wishy-washy about this leader business, it's because I can't state flatly that a 25-pound monofilament should be used for the butt end of a leader for a No. 9 fly line. Too much depends on which brand of monofilament is used, on the bug or fly to be cast, and on the particular fly line. It is better to proceed empirically.

To avoid compounding the problems of leader design, be sure to stick with the same brand of monofilament for all sections of the leader, except possibly for a short tippet made from a very limp line. The reason is that some monofilament lines are stiffer than others, and it is therefore entirely possible to have a 15-pound midsection that would be far stiffer than a 25-pound butt!

Anyhow, the important thing to remember when tying leaders for casting heavy lures is that the butt should be almost as stiff as the fly line. Then the stiffness should soften grudgingly on down to the tippet. Don't forget that stiffness and stiffness alone is the key to designing workable leaders for casting heavy lures, and, unfortunately, neither line diameter nor pound-test rating necessarily reflects stiffness. For this reason, I've always felt that anglers who use precision micrometers in tying leaders are just kidding themselves, unless visibility is their main interest.

Most of the regular monofilament on the market these days is soft (limber) because the manufacturers are catering to anglers who use the stuff on baitcasting gear as well as to spinning buffs. Although any good monofilament will work, I rather like the hard (stiff) monofilament leader material made by Mason and possibly other firms. But I do tie a short tippet made of soft monofilament onto this special leader line; a stiff tippet can kill the action of a bug or a streamer. It is difficult to find hard monofilament in tackle shops these days, but it is available from some of the mail order firms listed in the Appendix.

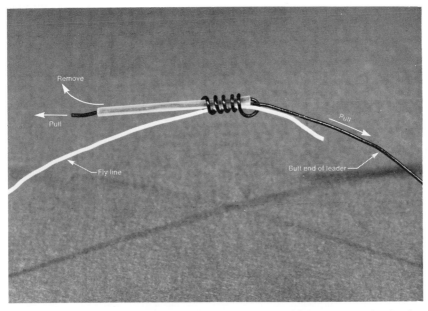

The nail knot is easier to tie if you use a tube, as shown here. The leader is wrapped around the fly line five or six times and is then run back under its own coils. Note that the fly line itself is stationary throughout the knotting process. After the knot is tightened, the ends should be trimmed closely.

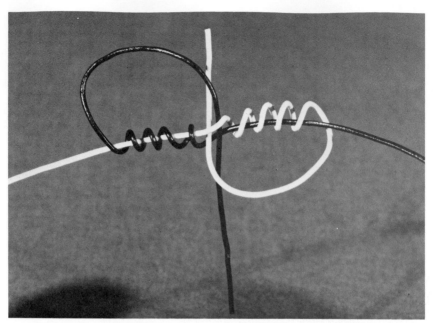

The blood knot is similar to two ordinary clinch knots.

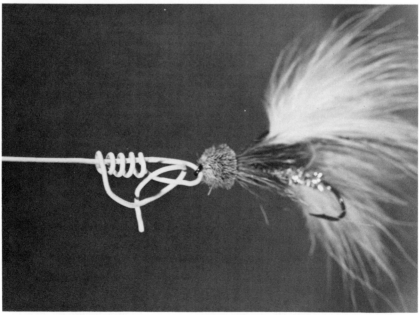

Improved clinch knot. For best results, draw this knot down smoothly.

Regardless of choice of monofilament, I join one length to another with the common blood knot. The butt end is attached to the fly line with a nail knot. Several firms market little barbed-wire eyelets that stick into the core of the fly line so that the leader can be attached with a clinch knot. I seldom use these myself; I simply don't trust them, and I doubt that they always transmit the energy properly from the fly line. But in all honesty I have not, during my limited experience with the things, had one of the eyelets pull out. On the other end of the leader, I always use the improved clinch knot to attach the hook eyelet to the tippet.

All the knots recommended here are shown in the illustrations on pages 39 and 40. I don't use the Palomar knot because I don't like the way the thing looks when it is drawn down. Other anglers swear that it is better than the improved clinch knot, and some expert fishermen insist that some sort of loop in the end of the line should be used with some flies. Flies tied on hooks with turned-down eyes seem to work better with an improved turtle knot, which gives the line a straight pull. I haven't illustrated this knot simply because bass anglers seldom use dry flies or other lures with turned-down hook eyes. (Anyone interested in knots should pick up a copy of *Practical Fishing Knots* by Lefty Kreh and Mark Sosin.)

If you don't want to tie your own leaders, you can purchase either hand-tied leaders or knotless tapered leaders made by machine. If you shop around, you can find a wide range of leaders from which to choose. Most of these ready-made leaders are classified according to a numbering system, keyed to butt diameter, tippet diameter, and tippet pound test. There is some variation from one brand to another, but the following table is typical:

Size	Butt Diameter (in inches)	Tippet Diameter (in inches)	Pound Test
3X	0.021	0.008	4
2X	0.021	0.009	5
1X	0.023	0.010	6
0X	0.023	0.011	7
9/5	0.025	0.012	10
8/5	0.025	0.013	12
7/5	0.029	0.014	14

Many of the tapered leaders come with a loop on the butt end. I don't care for these, but, admittedly, loops make it easy to change from one leader to another. Personally, I seldom change a whole leader, and I have fished for months with the same butt. I do, however, frequently change my tippet. This, in turn, soon inches away at the next link in the leader until it is too short and has to be replaced or extended. I strongly suspect that anglers who buy knotless tapered leaders soon have several knots in them anyhow, either by replacing tippets or because they have to cut out wind knots.

Whether you purchase tapered leaders or tie your own, it is advisable to take proper care of them, especially if you are using a light tippet in lunker country. Inspect the tippet and smaller portions of the leader frequently. Nicks and abrasions can often be detected by running the line (under slight tension) between thumb and forefinger. Do not keep spare leaders or leader materials in sunlight; ultraviolet rays will weaken monofilament.

Check your leader frequently for wind knots. A simple overhand knot can weaken monofilament line by as much as 50 percent.

Monofilament has what is called a property of memory. If it is coiled for any length of time, it will tend to return to the same coil when you are casting and fishing with it. Stretching the leader before a fishing trip will help, but the best is to rub the leader between rubber surfaces. Just cut a small piece of inner tube, fold it over between thumb and forefinger, and pull the line through it. Leonard's and other firms market special leader straightening pads, made from either rubber or leather.

Many of the better fly reels have a large-diameter spool and will accommodate quite a lot of backing line. Whether or not you expect to tie into a large fish, you should put on the correct amount of backing line so that the fly line will completely fill the spool. Having a full spool will not only make for a faster pickup retrieve but also reduce line coil.

Determining the exact amount of backing line is best done by first spooling on the fly line *leader end first*. Then attach the backing line with a nail knot and fill the spool within ⅛ inch or so of capacity. Next, tie the end of the backing line temporarily to a tree and walk off until you have stripped all the line from the reel. Then tie the end of the backing line to the reel arbor and respool. I attach the backing line (or the fly line if no backing line is used) to the spool as shown in the accompanying illustration.

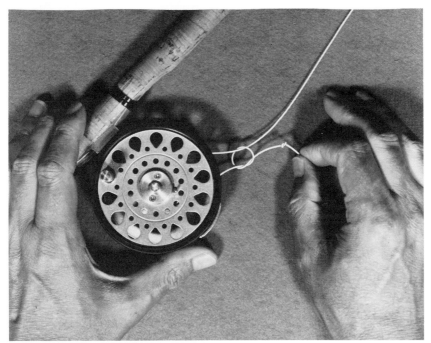

To attach a fly line or backing line to the reel, run the line around the arbor and tie an overhand knot in the tag end. Then tie another overhand knot around the standing line. Tighten and trim.

Any sort of backing line of suitable strength will do, but most experienced fly fishermen prefer 20-pound dacron. It has a very long life and low stretch. Any braided line will work, and many anglers use monofilament. If you do use monofilament, remember that it will stretch quite a lot. If you spool it on under tension, it can exert enough pressure to damage your reel spool.

Finally, the nail knot connecting the backing line to the fly line should be smooth so that it won't hang in one of the rod guides, which could someday cause you to lose a big fish. Tying the knot carefully, drawing it down slowly, and trimming it closely will help. It also helps to apply a drop of Pliobond cement, made by Goodyear.

4

Other Gear, Tackle, and Fishing Aids

POSSIBLY BECAUSE I HAVE a tricky back, I feel that the development of the bass boat is the greatest thing that has happened to the sport since the invention of the rod and reel. And, to me, it's even more important for fly-rodding from a boat than for using a baitcasting or spinning rig. Anyone who has ever worked an irregular shoreline with bass bugs for 8 hours from a 12-foot aluminum johnboat with slat seats will know what I mean.

The bass boat is a stable craft with a rather squared or rounded bow. It is fitted with pedestal easy seats instead of slat seats. Available in varying degrees of comfort, the seats should swivel 360 degrees freely, thereby permitting the angler to face his target without having to twist about. If you like to stand up to cast, consider a boat with elevated fishing decks and removable pedestal seats. The seats on these boats can be lifted out of a socket in seconds and can be put back in just as quickly.

Another requirement of the bass boat is that it have a flat surface up front on which to mount an electric motor. This surface must be flush with the bow.

44

The comfortable seats on a bass boat make fly-rodding more enjoyable. These anglers have hauled this boat a thousand miles to fish in Florida lakes.

There are now all manner of bass boats on the market, taking outboards of from 10 horsepower up to 150, and some are powered by inboard/outboard engines. A recent trend is toward high-performance boats, built on racing hulls. The more fancy boats, if fully rigged, can cost as much as $7,000. They are worth it if you do a lot of fishing and can afford such a boat. But look around carefully before buying, and make certain that you get a boat that suits your needs. If you plan to fish in the bass tournaments, some of which have purses into six figures, it would be wise to get a 17- or 18-foot rig with two large live wells. But if you don't fish tournaments, one live well will do fine. If you release your catch, you won't need even a single live well.

If you're interested in bass boats but don't know exactly what you want, the best bet is to attend a large boat show or visit several dealers to get some idea of what's available. There are, of course, some good bass-boat salesmen, but most of them aren't worth talking

to and will sell you something you don't need. Before buying, you
might take a look at my book *Advanced Bass Tackle and Boats*.

Whether or not you buy (or own) a full-fledged bass boat, you'll
catch more fish and enjoy it more by having an electric motor. Now
available in about a hundred models, these electrics are usually
called trolling motors, although very few bassmen actually troll with
them. Instead, they are fishing motors. The bassman uses them to
move the boat along slowly while he is casting to the shoreline or fishing out underwater structure. The motor should be mounted on the
bow of the boat, simply because the angler has better control than he
would have with a stern-mounted electric.

Most bass anglers prefer remote-controlled motors. These have a
foot pedal with which the angler can start and stop the motor as well
as control its direction of thrust. Thus, the angler has both hands free
for fishing. Some bassmen, however, prefer to have a manually
steered motor together with an unobtrusive foot switch mounted on
the fishing deck. This rig eliminates the cumbersome foot pedal, but it
requires the angler to steer the motor by hand or by nudging it with
his foot. I prefer a good foot-controlled unit, but the pedal can cause

*On this boat, the electric motor is mounted on the right side of the bow
and the foot-control unit is on the right forward fishing deck. The depth
finder is mounted on the console in front of the steering wheel.*

the fly-rodder some problems. It tangles his line. Even so, I've used a foot-controlled motor so long that handling the boat is almost automatic, and I feel that I am in better control of things with my foot on the pedal. I might add that I also use an electric motor when I am doing battle with a large fish. I can quickly swing the bow of the boat around one way or the other to help prevent a fish from getting under the boat, and I always head the boat away from the cover when I tie into a large bass with a light tippet.

All things considered, I believe that a foot-controlled electric motor has at least doubled my catch, and could well have tripled it. Incidentally, I was using a foot-controlled electric on boats of one sort or another long before I had a fancy bass boat.

Here are some other helpful items:

Depth finders and electronic aids. In my opinion, no bass boat is complete without at least one depth finder aboard. (Many anglers, myself included, use a second depth finder, mounted on the left side of the bow with its transducer attached to the shaft of the electric motor.) I prefer the permanent-mount type because it doesn't bounce around and because it operates from the boat's 12-volt battery system.

Although the fly-rodder will usually fish in rather shallow water, depth finders are still very helpful. If, for example, you're fishing the shoreline or visible cover in a submerged creek bottom of a man-made impoundment, you'll be more likely to catch a lunker bass where the old creek channel runs close to the cover. So you need to know where the creek channel is, whether or not you fish in it.

A good depth finder will cost well over $100, but it is worth it. Every penny. In addition to determining the depth of the water, a depth finder will locate underwater structure—and the expert can often tell whether the bottom is mud, sand, rock, or covered with vegetation merely by looking at his flasher's dial. The width and intensity of the signal is the key. The instruction manuals packed with the better depth finders give explanations of the various signals and what they might mean. Practice, however, is necessary.

A flasher depth finder is highly desirable because it shows multiple signals. But other types are available as second units. Chart recorders are great for detailed mapping of submerged structure, but they are a little slow for on-the-spot fishing. Both flashers and chart recorders will show suspended fish, and most firms that make and sell them call them fish finders. This is misleading. Most bassmen use them only to determine the depth of the water and the characteristics of the lake bottom. In other words, they use a depth finder to look for likely bass habitat, not to find bass swimming around in the lake.

If you buy a new depth finder and have trouble with it, make sure that the transducer is mounted correctly before you send the unit back. Cavitation or air bubbles from the boat's hull, or electrical interference from the outboard, can cause erratic signals, and can even cause the signals to disappear from the dial. I prefer transducers that mount permanently to the boat, either on the transom or in a well inside the boat. There are some rather steady clamp-on brackets for transducers, but I would advise anyone to avoid brackets held on by suction cups.

Many bass anglers have hand-held temperature indicators. These are worked by lowering a weighted probe into the water, and then reading the temperature on a dial. The probe line is color-coded, so that the angler can easily correlate depth and temperature. Some bassmen also mount continuous-reading surface-temperature meters on their bass boats; these can give readings while the boat is running across the lake, and they are very convenient.

Light-intensity meters and oxygen monitors are also available. These are hand-held units, and they work like the temperature probes.

Light meters have limited application to fly-fishing, and, frankly, I've never used mine while I was after bass. I do, however, experiment with it from time to time, and I feel that I am a more knowledgeable angler for it. (Some results of my efforts are set forth in Chapter 10.)

Oxygen monitors are in my opinion valuable gadgets for any serious bass angler to have, but the fly-rodder can certainly get along without one. As I see it, oxygen monitors are more useful for fishing in deep water. I don't use my oxygen monitor too often when I'm fishing for bass, but I do like to have it aboard my boat. I don't run around the lake looking for hot spots with ideal oxygen content, but I do use it sometimes to help eliminate fishless waters. For example, I once caught a large bass from the bottom of a 35-foot hole near my home, and thereafter I spent many hours fishing for another one in the same hole. When I obtained an oxygen monitor, I made a quick check and was surprised to see that there wasn't enough oxygen on the bottom to support bass. Since then, I've saved myself a lot of time. When I want to fish the hole, or some similar spot, I first make a quick reading. If the oxygen is low, I move on. If it's right, I fish with more confidence. And it takes only a few minutes to check.

Bass pro Ricky Green takes a reading with an oxygen monitor.

Maps. A contour map of a lake or impoundment can be very valuable to a bass angler. A good hydrological map will help, but in some cases a set of very detailed topographic maps can be obtained from the U.S. Geological Survey. To obtain information about maps of specific impoundments, write to the Map Information Office, U.S. Geological Survey National Center, Sunrise Valley Drive, Reston, Virginia 22092. Be certain to mention that you are interested in fishing the impoundment and would therefore need a map showing man-made structure as well as contour lines. In some cases, new topographic maps do not show such features, and copies of older maps are more useful, if they are available. There are also some commercial contour maps and even atlases of some lakes and impoundments.

Although I don't recommend that the fly-rodder seek out submerged structure in more than 25 feet of water, I do recommend that he be thoroughly familiar with the water depth of a lake or impoundment. Quite often bass, especially the larger ones, will be in cover or structure near deep water. So a good map can help you whether or not you fish deep.

Waders. Although I've waded around the edges of some lakes, and in some streams, in nothing but jeans and sneakers, I feel better using chest-high waders. Some of these have boot feet; others have stocking feet and are intended for wear under a separate set of shoes, boots, or sandals. Strap-on devices with cleats or other special gripping aids are available. My personal choice is boot waders with felt soles. In addition to its nonslip properties, felt permits the angler to move quietly. Whichever sort of waders you choose, buy good ones and take care of them.

Hip boots will do for very shallow wading, but I usually end up getting wet when I use them. Frankly, I believe that hip boots are much more dangerous than waders if you should step into deep or swift water. Waders are pretty safe, provided that you wear a belt around them at the waist. The belt will prevent the waders from quickly filling with water, whereas there's nothing to prevent hip boots from filling. On the other hand, it's easier to get out of hip boots.

Tubes. Truck-size inner tubes fitted with a fabric cover and seat rather split the difference between wading and fishing from a boat. In cool weather, or when fishing a relatively cold smallmouth stream, most anglers use the tube along with waders so that they won't get wet.

Tubes are often used as an aid in wading streams. Normally, the angler keeps his feet on the bottom, but uses the tube to drift over deep holes.

Tubes are also frequently used in ponds and lakes. The angler can propel himself by using a small paddle, but it's best, in my opinion, to wear rubber flapper-type swimming fins or special tube fins made of metal. The latter are fitted with hinges so that the fin will straighten out when the angler moves his foot forward; when he moves it backward, the fin hinges back 90 degrees, thereby creating forward thrust. It's rather like walking through the water.

Some fabric tube covers are fitted with tackle and gear compartments, and others have vertical rod holders. The rod holders aren't of much help to the fly-rodder, but a tackle compartment comes in handy.

Fishing vests. Wading all day in a stream without a good fishing vest is almost like hiking overnight without a good backpack. Modern fishing vests have pockets all over them, inside and out, with pockets on pockets and under pockets, and will hold an amazing

Fishing vests come in handy for fishing streams. This angler is working a Vermont stream.

amount of tackle, leaders, flies, insect repellent, and the like. For short trips up or down a stream, however, a vest is not necessary for bass fishing. Extra tippet material, clippers, and a few bugs or streamers are all one needs. Cliché or not, I put extra bugs and flies on my straw hat.

Although the biggest danger on most streams is in slipping down in very shallow water, anglers unaccustomed to wading may be uneasy about getting in over their heads. If so, I suggest that they look into flotation fishing vests.

Tackle boxes. Streamers and bucktails can be kept in fly books, which have "pages" of felt, wool, or some similar material. The hook's point can be stuck into the page a bit to help keep the flies in order. These books work fine with even large streamers and bucktails, but not with bugs and such flies as the muddler, which have more body.

Bass bugs are best kept in compartments. There are some plastic boxes designed to hold such things, but frankly I prefer an ordinary tackle box with wide compartments. I have some very large bugs with rubber legs, and I don't like to squeeze them into a small place. If you do most of your fishing from a boat, I would advise you to get a large tackle box so that you'll have plenty of room for extra reel spools, tippet material, and so on. Then, if you should wade a stream, you can get out what you think you'll need.

If you fish with soft plastic worms and other such lures, be sure to get a box that's "worm proof." Worm material will melt or "burn" some plastic boxes. And be *sure* to keep your worms separate—isolated— unless you want your pretty flies and bugs to end up a sticky, wretched mess. Plastic worm bags are highly advisable.

Landing nets. I seldom use a landing net for bass. Instead, I work them up close and grasp the lower jaw with thumb and forefinger. If you do use a landing net, get one that's big enough, and don't try to scoop up a lunker bass with a net that is narrower than the fish is long. I've caught a number of bass that were over 26 inches long, which means that a 30-inch net wouldn't be too large. More bass, I'd say, have been lost during the last moments of the battle than at any other time simply because the excited angler, or his fishing companion, tried to scoop them up in a small net. I would also recommend a net with wide mesh, and one made from green or brown nylon cording. A white net suddenly stuck into the water, or swatted down, will sometimes scare a lunker bass into one last lunge, and this can be disastrous at close quarters.

In any case, it's best to land your own lunker without help from a fishing partner. At least, that's the way I feel about it.

Stripping baskets. Most fly-rodders keep some line off the reel, and those who shoot for distance keep a lot off. Stepping on this line can ruin it, and tangles can foul up a shooting cast. Instead of having this line loose on the boat deck, or in the water if the angler is wading, some anglers prefer a stripping basket, which they strap around the waist with a belt. Such baskets are available from some of the specialty houses listed in the Appendix. Before you buy one, however, remember that it is pretty hard to keep a line in a stripping basket. If you aren't very careful, part of the line will flop over the side, and this part will often pull the rest out.

Polarized sunglasses. Besides cutting glare and making the day's outing more pleasant, good polarized sunglasses will help you catch more bass. This is especially true in shallow, clear water. I personally don't think it is sporting to stalk bass when they're bedding, but if you want to try it, polarized glasses will certainly help you spot the beds.

They will also help you keep your eye on your bug, and this can be important. Seeing the bass strike will help you react quicker, and the quicker you react the better will be your chances of setting the hook.

Part Two

Lures and How to Fish Them

ALL MANNER OF BUGS and streamers and other lures are discussed in the following chapters. I would like at this point to make a couple of comments that will apply to any fly-rod lure. First, most bugs and some flies are sold with hooks that are not properly sharpened. Always inspect the point of a hook, new or old, before fishing with it. The larger the hook, the sharper it should be. Be especially critical of the heavy-duty hooks used for some bugs and streamers that were made primarily for saltwater use.

Second, look at the hook eyelet on your bugs. Most manufacturers dip their bugs into lacquer; consequently, the eyelet is likely to be clogged up. Some firms and tiers apparently drill holes through this paint, which can leave a hard, sharp edge that will cut and abrade your monofilament tippet. Always clean all the paint from in and around an eyelet. On old bugs, watch out for rust in the eyelet. A rough or rusty eyelet can abrade the tippet when the angler draws the knot down.

Third, a lot of bassmen err by buying a bug so heavy and wind-resistant that they can't cast it with normal fly gear. The size of the hook is by no means the only criterion, but, in general, I wouldn't recommend any lure—feather, hair, or cork—tied on a hook larger than a 1/0. The weight of the bug or lure isn't the only consideration, but it is a fundamental one. Using a bug that is too heavy for the fly line will hold back the cast, just as using a *line* that is too heavy will hold back the cast in spinning or baitcasting. You can't cast a ¼-ounce spinning plug with a 60-pound monofilament line. Nor can you cast a heavy 3/0 fly-rod bug with a No. 6 line.

In the chapters that follow, I have generally avoided the subject of lure color. It is, however, pretty well established that the black bass can distinguish between some colors, and it is widely believed that bass will often show preference for one color or another. The best bet is to stock up with a variety of colors and switch about until you find something that is hot for the day. For openers, you might try light colors in clear water, dark colors in dark water; light colors in shallow water, dark in deep; light during midday, dark early in the morning and late in the afternoon. In any case, look at the bottom of surface lures to see what color you're actually fishing with. All the pretty colors and eyes put on the top of a bug are not seen by a bass, unless the bug turns upside down in the water. Not long ago I was fishing with a fellow who said he thought he'd try a frog pattern. His bug did look rather like a frog on top, but on the bottom it was plain yellow!

5

Fishing on Top

IF I WERE A POET, I would probably begin this chapter by praising the beauties of a lake or stream at sunrise or sunset, or by painting the picture of a lone angler only vaguely seen on a misty morning—but fishing a bass bug at such times is likely to elicit such an eruption in the calm waters that the fly-rodder will quickly forget to observe the qualities of the day! In my opinion, there is no greater thrill in angling than a bass (or a snook) smashing a surface bug.

Yet bugs and other surface lures are not always the best bet for taking bass. Most of the bass caught on a fly rod are, to be sure, hooked on the surface, but this is because that's where most fly-rodders fish. Generally, bass hit surface lures better in early morning, late afternoon, at night, and on cloudy or rainy days. And nearly always in shallow water. A bass will not often rise from 20 feet down to hit a surface lure, no matter how skillfully it is played. Consequently, the fly-rodder can usually catch a more hefty stringer of bass by going deeper during the heat of the day. But there are exceptions, and I've caught 8-pound bass on surface lures at midday in clear water under a bright sun. These exceptions occur just often enough to hold me

These anglers are fishing in the dawn mist on Georgia's Lake Lewis.

along a shoreline or grass bed long after I should have headed for deeper waters. The plain truth is that fishing on the surface is more fun. It's also much easier.

Although deer-hair bugs have been around for some time, the first cork bugs were made by E. H. Peckinpaugh in the early 1900s. Most of the bugs on the market today are still made from cork, but hard plastic bugs are not uncommon. I prefer balsa bugs over either cork or plastic because they seem to be a little more bouncy in the water, but the material doesn't lend itself to mass production and balsa bugs are therefore not commonly available in tackle shops or from mail-order houses.

Before discussing the various bug designs, I would like to point out two rather basic errors to avoid when selecting a bass bug. First, many bassmen fail to understand that the larger the bug the harder it is to cast; consequently, they tend to buy large bugs that cannot be cast easily with normal bass rods and line. Second, many bugs on the market—and especially those with fat bodies—will not hook fish as often as they should. Remember that a bug's body is fitted around the hook's shank, and this can result in a lure that doesn't have enough "bite." A bug should be made on a long shank hook, and the point should be well behind the end of the bug's body. The hooking properties of an ill-designed bug can be improved by springing the point out somewhat—but this reduces the hook's holding power.

Unlike trout and salmon flies, bass bugs haven't been endlessly patterned, variegated, named, and catalogued. Although manufacturers and individual craftsmen have given names to their creations, the important designs depend not so much on dressings of hair and feathers but on the shape of the bug's body. Thus, there are several *types* of bass bug, and these are discussed below along with some other surface lures and flies:

Poppers. These highly popular bugs have a hollow, dished-out face designed to cause a pop, or plop, when the angler twitches the rod tip or hauls in line with a little jerk. There is a certain sound to a good popper, and it's the sonic thing that arouses bass. Or so it seems. The popper doesn't merely push water spray ahead, and doesn't merely create a ruckus on the surface of the water. If I see it correctly, the face of a good popper plunges downward, creating air bubbles and directing a sort of acoustical blast into the water. It is, of course, possible to pop a bug too loudly, and I believe that many bass anglers err in this direction, especially in shallow water. At times a very gentle

Popping bug by Boone. Note the dished-out face.

plop may be required to coax a bass to hit. On the other hand, a popper worked fast and furious will sometimes trigger strike responses when all else fails. As a general rule, I pop a bug loudly at night or in dark water, more gently in clear water; loudly in water deeper than 4 or 5 feet, more gently in shallow water.

Apart from the loudness of the pop, a bug can be fished slow or fast. The question is how long to wait between pops. Erratic retrieves will of course catch bass, but a more studied approach usually works best for me. My favorite method of fishing a popper is first to present it gently on the cast and then wait until the waves dissipate before popping it. Then wait again until the ripples dissipate before making the second pop. And so on for five or six pops. Then pick up and recast to another spot. The reasoning behind this retrieve is that the pops hold the bass's attention and the long pauses play on its curiosity and patience. Another tactic is to twitch the bug slightly. Twitch it again a little harder. Then pop it lightly. Then continue with a series of pops that are progressively more vigorous and closer together in time. The idea behind this retrieve is that the bug falls into the water, is stunned, slowly recovers, and makes away. This retrieve can also be used with other surface lures, and has taken many a bass for pluggers.

Popping bugs can cause some severe casting problems. Weight and air resistance are factors with any bass bug, and poppers further complicate casting because they create a lot of resistance on the pickup. Some even tend to dive. The trick is to start the bug moving along the surface before it is picked up; make it take off like an airplane. The actual lift-off should not occur until the rod is at an angle of about 45 degrees; the elevated rod tip, together with the increasing speed, will make the bug come up smoothly instead of diving or popping. What's more, sliding the bug along the surface will sometimes trigger a strike from a bass that had ignored the pop-and-rest routine. In fact, it's not a bad idea to *fish* the bug during the pickup.

By contrast, some anglers jerk their bugs out of the water and thereby cause enough ruckus to lower their chances of catching a bass on subsequent casts in the vicinity. Not long ago I fished behind such a fellow in a bass boat. We were casting down the edge of a long grass bank late in the afternoon. Quite correctly, he wanted his bug within inches of the grass, or exactly in a foot-wide pocket. But this guy would sometimes make three or four casts, slash and thrash, before he got his bug exactly where he wanted it, and each time he made a short cast he would immediately snatch the bug out of the water and angrily plop it back. The more he worked at it, the worse he got. It would have been better for him, and for me, if he had fished out his bum casts instead of frothing the water. We didn't catch many bass, although at other times I had consistently taken limits of bass along the same grass bed.

Anyhow, poppers are great bugs for bass if they are correctly used. They are ideal for fishing out pockets in lily pads or for casting to stumps and similar cover. Water resistance prevents the bug from moving far when it is popped, and, consequently, the angler can keep the bug in the pocket instead of pulling it out. At the other extreme, poppers are not ideal for covering a lot of water fast, so that the complete bassman will have other bugs in his box.

Pushers. Although some bugs of this type are called poppers, and will pop, they don't have hollow faces and don't have quite the same sonic effect. They will create bubbles on the surface and have good visual appeal, but they don't trap as much air and direct it downward into the water. Hence, they may not be as good as poppers for attracting bass from some distance away.

Balsa pushers by Poul Jorgensen and Bill Gallasch.

I usually fish pushers pretty much the same way as poppers, but in a different frame of mind. I think of them as imitations of something (such as a frog) going through the water with steady, stop-and-go, lunging strokes. In any case, pushers can be worked faster than poppers and lend themselves better to a fast, zigzag retrieve.

A lot of pusher bodies are longer and thinner than poppers, but a few, such as the Gerbubble Bug, are flattened instead of rounded. Weight and air resistance being equal, pushers are easier to pick up and therefore cast a little better.

Spouters. These bugs, which are not as common as poppers or pushers, cause spouts of water to shoot up in the air on the retrieve. They have an irregular face that is hard to describe. The face is a sort of slanted triangle dished out on either side. As Bill Gallasch put it in one of his price lists, the face is "sort of half moon shaped from the center of the bug." (See the drawing on page 63.)

I haven't fished extensively with spouters because they aren't commonly available in tackle shops. But they have caught bass for me, and the action looks good. The significance of the water spouts is

Top row: Popper designs. The bug on the left, without a slanted face, tends to dive.

Bottom row: A pusher (left) doesn't have a dished-out face. A slider (middle) has a pointed face. A spouter (right) has a triangulated face.

  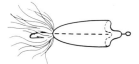

not entirely clear to me, but, hell, it's something different—and that alone might sometimes be enough to do the trick!

Sliders. These bugs have pointed or bullet-shaped faces and therefore create less surface ruckus than poppers, pushers, or spouters. They are ideal for fast retrieves in lunging or zigzag patterns, and they can also be effective with slow, twitch-and-rest retrieves. If they are rigged with hook guards, they are very good for fishing in weeds and grass because they don't get snagged as readily as snub-nosed bugs.

Rubber-skirted bugs. Most of the bass bugs made with cork, balsa, or plastic bodies are dressed with feathers or hair. A few, however, such as the Arbogast Hula Poppers, are fitted with rubber skirts. These can be very effective. The secret is in the action of the skirt when the bug is dead in the water. If the skirt is working properly, the strands of rubber will move about on their own, slowly curling outward and upward. The way to take advantage of this enticing movement is to pause 30 seconds between pops or twitches.

It is important that the rubber skirt be of top quality and in good condition. It must seem alive in the water; a dead skirt just doesn't have that subtle, enticing movement. I suppose that long storage in general is bad for a skirt, but the quickest way to kill one is to store it in a hot place or to overexpose it to sunlight. Also, the paint on some lures apparently reacts chemically with the rubber skirt, causing a half-melted, tangled mess. The best bet is to store skirts

Hula Popper by Fred Arbogast, a champion of rubber skirts. Note that this skirt seems alive, even in a still photograph. Dead skirts should be replaced.

(dry) in plastic bags or in a small bottle of distilled water. A pork jar will do nicely.

Many of the spinnerbaits and other bass lures are being fitted with plastic skirts these days. Although plastic skirts are easier to keep in good shape and work nicely enough on fast-moving lures, it is my opinion that rubber works best for slowly fished surface lures.

Rubber skirts can be purchased in most tackle shops, and I often buy them to fit on old bass bugs with unraveling hackle or hair. First, I remove all the hackle or hair with a razor blade. Then I thread the skirt onto the hook and snug it up to the body of the bug. Then, working from the rear, I wedge the skirt tight with trimmed matchsticks or toothpicks. Another method is to trim off some of the old hackle or hair, leaving enough body to wedge the skirt properly.

Rubber-legged bugs. Approximately half the bugs on the market have rubber legs, normally three or four off either side of the body. I usually prefer those with legs, especially when I am fishing where there is a slight ripple on the water, because I believe that they help hold a bass's attention. Another point: rubber legs help balance a bug in the water, whereas some bugs without legs tend to turn over on the retrieve, thereby causing the leader to twist. On the other hand, rubber legs add both weight and air resistance to a bug.

One problem with rubber legs is that they either tear off, mat, or become stiff with age. Much depends on having good rubber hackle to begin with, and then on storing the bugs properly. It is possible to replace rubber legs on cork or balsa bugs by using a needle, but whenever I have problems with legs I merely snip them off flush with the body and then use the bug without legs.

Hair bugs. Hair from deer, caribou, and elk is hollow, thereby making it ideal for tying floating bass bugs. The body of a hair bug is generally tied with a lot of hair, and the unfinished lure looks like a blob. Then the hair is trimmed down so that the thing resembles a frog, a moth, a mouse, or whatever.

The main point in favor of hair bugs is that they are lighter than those made of cork, balsa, or plastic. In spite of high wind resistance large hair bugs can be cast relatively easily. They also hit the water a bit more gently than most other bugs. In short, hair bugs are good choices for tough casting conditions, but they can't entirely replace cork or balsa bugs. Another point in favor of hair bugs is that they last longer, if they are well made.

Hair bugs can be fished pretty much the same way as poppers or pushers. Twitch and rest, twitch and rest. Slowly. But be sure to try the frogs and mice on a run-and-rest retrieve; that is, move them by hauling in line, so that the lure runs for 6 inches to a foot, then rest for a few seconds. Also try a slow, steady retrieve.

It is possible to alter the action of hairbugs by using fly or line dressing. As Charles Waterman pointed out in the January 1975 issue of *Florida Wildlife:* "If you want them to pop loudly, don't put any dressing on them. If you want the top part to stand up high and the lower part to get a little waterlogged and pop a little, dope the upper section with line dressing. If you want them to stand up and just dance on the surface, dope the whole works." Another tactic that can

This large hair moth, tied by Poul Jorgensen, is very light for its size.

be deadly is to fish a waterlogged hair bug with a slow, steady retrieve; being waterlogged, the bug will be almost under the surface and the retrieve will produce a heavy wake.

A semiweedless lure can be devised by tying the bug so that the point of the hook is flush with the hair body. This will cause the angler to miss some strikes, but it will often produce more strikes by enabling the angler to fish in lily pads, weeds, and other cover.

Muddlers. The muddler minnow and its variations are also made from deer hair and can be fished either wet or dry, depending on whether or not the body is waterlogged. If you want to fish a muddler on the surface, it should be doped; otherwise, it will have to be dried out often by false casting.

When fished dry, a muddler will create a buglike ruckus on the surface, and it can be effective when fished with a slow, steady retrieve. I am fond of fishing an undressed muddler on top for a few twitches or "pops," then letting it sink slowly, twitching it slightly as it goes down. Usually, I fish the muddler all the way to the bottom, then hop it along for several feet.

Muddlers and variations by Dan Bailey. This is probably the most versatile fly-rod lure ever devised.

If I had to choose one lure for all my fly-fishing, it would surely be a muddler. They are the most versatile of all fly-rodding lures.

Sponge spiders. Small spiders made of sponge rubber and rubber legs are terrific for bluegills, and they will also catch bass, especially in the larger sizes. For bluegills, they should be fished very slowly, letting them sit dead in the water for 30 seconds or even longer; for bass, however, they should be fished much faster, in my experience. Foot-long hauls can be effective, but I usually cast them out and fish them on a slow pickup. I once hit on this retrieve when winding in my line at the end of a bluegill session, and again when trolling my line behind the boat while I was rolling myself a cigarette!

But I seldom tie on a spider for bass—at least not especially for bass. When I'm after bluegills, however, I'll often use a spider for both bluegills and bass. The trick is to fish the spider very slowly for bluegills, then fish for bass with a sliding pickup.

Sputterbuzzers. Many surface plugs and other lures made for bass fishing with baitcasting or spinning gear have some sort of surface sputtering or bubbling spinner blade on them. To my knowl-

edge, the only lure of this type that is suitable for fly-rodding is the
Scrappy, made by Marathon Tackle. It has a cork body with a bucktail on the rear and a propeller-type spinner up front. I've had good
luck with this lure, but it is a bit heavy and difficult to cast. I fish it
with a twitch-and-rest retrieve, or with a fast, steady retrieve. Often
I'll cast this lure near a grass bed or shoreline while running the
electric motor on the boat. The moving boat actually trolls the lure,
but after it gets 3 or 4 feet from the cover I pick up and recast.

Buzzing lures can be devised by putting a Colorado spinner of
suitable size in front of sliders, pushers, and other surface lures.

Spinnerbaits have become quite popular in bass fishing, and many
anglers buzz them across the surface. The same effect can be achieved
with a fly rod by putting a small jig spinner onto a tiny jig. This lure
requires a fast retrieve to keep it up buzzing at the surface, and the

Sputtering bug by Marathon (left) and spouter by Bill Gallasch (right).

easiest method is to simply cast (or lob) it out and fish it on the pickup. This is a great lure for fishing out a lot of water fast, but it is so heavy that it is difficult to cast.

Miniature plugs. One of the best bass catchers available to bait-casting and spinning buffs is a balsa or plastic plug that can be twitched about on the surface, then pulled under for a wiggle re-trieve. Although a few plugs such as the 2-inch floating Rapala can be used on a fly rod, most plugs on the market are simply too heavy. It is, however, not too terribly difficult to make balsa lures, and some of the better baitcasting plugs, such as the original Big-O, are carved by hand. Anyone interested in making balsa lures should go to the library and look up an article called "Balsa, Fly Rod, and Bass" in the August 1974 issue of *Field & Stream.* This article gives how-to information plus detailed blueprints for several lures, including div-ing plugs and imitations of the Devil's Horse-type stick plugs. Back issues of *BASSmaster Magazine* also carried how-to articles for balsa plugs.

One problem with miniature plugs, in addition to weight, is that the treble hooks—especially the belly treble—cause the lure to tangle too frequently in the fly line or leader. Remember that the line and leader form a loop during the cast, and that the fly (or lure) must turn over at the end of the cast. Anyhow, if you want to try any lure with treble hooks, the tangle problem can be held to a minimum by using a hefty fly rod, an appropriate line, and a short, heavy leader. But note that a heavy tippet can kill the action of a balsa plug, so that using a tiny split ring in the lure eyelet would be ad-visable.

Although tiny plugs *can* be used on a fly rod, I feel that they are more suited to ultralight spinning rigs.

Dry flies. Smallmouth, redeyes, and other bass can be caught on dry flies, but the angler would usually do better (much better) with bugs and other lures. It's a matter of visibility, I think. In addition to their small size, most flies tied for trout sit on the surface film instead of actually in the water. Unless bass are actively feeding on a hatch, they aren't likely to notice such dainty offerings from any distance away, and, of course, dry flies aren't attractors because they don't create the surface ruckus associated with poppers and other bugs.

On the other hand, dry flies can be presented very softly, and this might be an unexplored application for the larger dry flies, especially when you are casting to skittish bass in shallow water. I suggest that anglers who tie their own flies experiment with large parachute patterns, which sit in the water instead of on the surface film.

Soft plastic lures. All manner of bugs and frogs and things are molded from soft plastic. Some of these lures will float if they are used with small, light hooks. And they will catch lots of bass. I seldom use them myself, however, because they tear too easily or too often twist around on the hook. On the other hand, a bass will hold these lures longer than it will a mouthful of cork and feathers; consequently, a soft plastic frog or something similar might be a good choice for the fly-rodder who forgets to keep a tight line or who fails to keep an eye on his bug!

6

Running Shallow

THE ULTIMATE IN FLY-RODDING for bass is the thrill of a lunker striking a bug on top of the water. But if the bass won't come up, the angler should be prepared to go down. Often this is merely a matter of tying a sinking lure onto the tippet without changing the floating line. If the angler intends to fish deeper than about 5 feet, however, he should use a sinking line or a sinking tip.

Most of the wet flies and streamers on the market are tied for trout and just aren't large enough for bass, unless you're after redeyes and other species that don't average much more than a pound in weight. Small lures will, to be sure, catch some bass of any sort—but I firmly believe that day in and day out the bass angler will do better to fish No. 2 and larger flies. I prefer streamers at least 4 inches long for largemouth bass and usually also for smallmouth. The larger flies and lures are easier for bass to see, and they make more vibrations, or stronger ones, on the retrieve. I might add that every bass has a large mouth for its size.

But smallmouth and other basses will at times show a preference for small fare, as when the water is colder than normal and their metabolism lower, or when they are intent on a school of small bait-fish. So, if you've got a bunch of trout flies, don't hesitate to try them in bass waters, especially if you don't mind catching lots of small bass, bluegills, and such.

Trout flies, small streamers, and nymphs can be made to look larger by attaching some sort of trailer to them. I prefer thin, narrow pork rind, but strips of plastic and rubber from balloons, torn plastic raincoats, and such material as surveyor's flagging can be used. I suppose that trout snobs will ruffle their hackles mightily at the very idea of hanging a strip of pork onto a beautiful fly, but the bass don't seem to mind. Maybe they think it's an eel or something chasing a fly.

In any case, no fly-rodder after bass should be without a good selection of subsurface lures. Here's my breakdown:

Streamers and bucktails. Both streamers and bucktails are generally intended to imitate minnows, whereas wet and dry flies are tied to imitate some sort of insect. There are exceptions, and streamerlike lures can be tied in the likeness of eels, leeches, sirens, and so on; but at least 95 percent of the commercially made streamers and bucktails are minnow imitations and should be fished as such. The difference between streamers and bucktails is mostly in the materials. Streamers have feather wings, and bucktails are made entirely from hair. Bucktails are usually more serviceable than streamers, but of course a good deal depends on the quality of the workmanship.

Any of the streamer or bucktail patterns will catch bass. The saltwater patterns that I've tried were excellent, and were large enough to interest even lunker largemouth bass. Note, however, that saltwater flies are usually tied on large, heavy hooks, which should therefore be kept very sharp.

My favorite way to work a streamer or bucktail is to alternate short hauls with pauses. But experiment. Fast and slow. Rhythmically and erratically. One trick is to weight the head with lead wire, so that the streamer has an up-and-down motion on the retrieve; I've found this jiglike motion to be very effective with long, flowing, eel-like streamers. Streamers and bucktails are also effective when used with a spinner attachment. The spinner blade imparts a tight wiggle to the wings. (Spinners are discussed at some length under a separate heading.) I feel, however, that too many bass anglers impart too much action to streamers and bucktails, especially when they are

Large streamers by Poul Jorgensen. These were tied for saltwater use, but the author likes to use them for big bass.

fishing streams. A streamer or bucktail merely sinking down naturally is often deadly on bass.

One of the most effective streamers is the "breather," designed so that the wing feathers curve out. If it is properly tied, it does indeed seem to breathe in and out when retrieved in short hauls. Work it very slowly.

The marabou patterns can be almost irresistible when fished slowly. At their best, marabou streamers have a subtle, enticing action; at worst, they merely mat. Apparently a good deal depends on the tier's acumen in selecting the right part of the plume.

Also see my discussion of the Muddler Minnow in Chapter 5 and of the weedless keel-hook streamers and bucktails in Chapter 8.

Wet flies. All of the larger wet flies will take bass, but they aren't quite as productive, day in and day out, as the streamers and bucktails. Wet flies are shorter and don't have the same action. But they can be quite effective when fished as such, or when used with a spinner and a thin, narrow pork strip. The length of the pork strip isn't critical, but I prefer mine to be about 1½ times the length of the fly. If the pork strip is a thick one, I take a razor blade and make a splittail out of it.

Nymphs. Forget them. Most of these are tied on very small hooks and just aren't large enough for bass. Although I have caught a 7-pound bass on a No. 10 Montana nymph while I was fishing for bluegills, I consider this to be a fluke. I think the nymph just sank down in front of the bass's nose, and maybe it sucked the nymph into its big mouth while yawning.

Spinner attachments. Spinners can be used with any of the streamers, bucktails, and wet flies, as well as with pork rind, plastic lures, and rubber skirts.

Hildebrandt and other firms make spinners in all sizes, including some that are small enough for flies. It's best to more or less match the spinner size to the lure, but the size of the spinner blade isn't the only consideration. Shapes and design variations can also be important.

There are several shapes of spinner blade, but the ones most commonly used on bass tackle are the Colorado, Indiana, French, and willowleaf. There is, however, a good deal of variation in blades of various manufacture, so that it is difficult, in some cases, to classify a particular blade as either a Colorado or an Indiana. The important thing to remember is that the shape determines how the blade acts. Generally, a wide blade turns slower and swings wider; a narrow blade turns faster and at a narrow angle to the axis. A wide blade starts turning at a slower speed; a narrow blade, at a faster speed. A wide blade has more resistance in the water and therefore tends to make the lure rise; a narrow blade has less resistance and allows the lure to run deeper. Thus, a Colorado blade is a good choice if you want to buzz a lure slowly along the surface, whereas a willowleaf blade is a good choice if you want to fish a lure rather fast along the bottom.

Spinner blade shapes

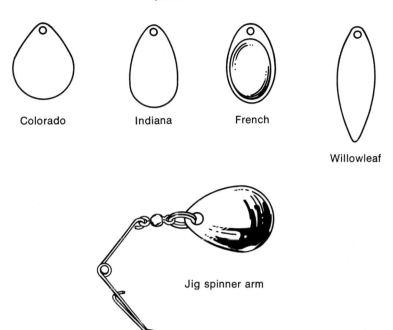

Colorado   Indiana   French   Willowleaf

Jig spinner arm

But shape isn't the only consideration. The size of the blade, the thickness of the metal, and the degree of dishing all have an effect on the resistance of the blade in the water. Also, a smooth blade has less resistance than a hammered or a fluted blade.

Although I personally feel that sonic effect and vibration are more important than flash, most anglers think of spinners only in terms of color and reflection. Traditionally, spinner blades have been finished in copper, gold, brass, nickel, and chrome. A few silver-plated spinner blades are made, but, as far as I can determine, they are available in this country only on the Mepps lures. According to the Mepps people, and I agree with them, silver does have more flash.

In addition to the metallic finishes, painted spinner blades are becoming more and more popular with bass anglers. I've seen red, yellow, white, black, and various fluorescent shades. I might add that it's not necessary to stock all colors. One can give a cast to most spinner blades by using permanent-ink felt-tip markers. The marker ink works well enough when thoroughly dry, but I personally don't like the "alcohol" smell. On the other hand, I understand that good bourbon whiskey is a bass attractor!

Doglegged jig spinners can be used for fly-rodding, but jigs themselves are awfully heavy for their size. I have attached jig spinners to regular unweighted streamers and bucktails with the aid of a small intermediate split ring; this rig will catch bass, but the spinner arm rides down and can't be used satisfactorily for surface buzzing. If the spinner arm is to ride up, a good bit of weight has to be added to the fly.

Spinner flies. A few flies are manufactured with a small propeller-type spinner up front. They'll catch bass, especially when a pork trailer is used with them. One trick is to raise the rod tip sharply as soon as the fly touches down; this will buzz the surface, and may thereby get a bass's attention. After the short spurt on the surface, let the fly sink down, then retrieve it with fast, foot-long hauls. (If you fish it very slowly, you'll have trouble keeping crappie off your line!)

Swimming flies. Best Tackle Company markets a swimming bucktail, called the Stanley Streamer, that has a plastic lip fitted into the head. It comes in several sizes, and in some beautiful colors. The action is very good, and it is the only fly that swims and wiggles like a plug on the retrieve. The objection that I have is that the Stanley Streamer is rather difficult to get out of the water. This makes the pickup awkward and gets the backcast off to a bad start. It is, however, great for trolling.

Soft plastic lures. Worms are by far the most popular and productive bass lures for spinning and baitcasting, and the smaller ones can be used with a fly rod, if somewhat clumsily. I have fished 6-inch "pencil" worms with a hefty fly rod and a No. 10 line, but they're a little heavy. The 4-inch worms work much better. Simply cast them out, let them sink, and retrieve them either by hauling in line, by subtle twitches of the rod tip, or by raising the rod tip slowly so that the worm moves about 4 feet and then settles down again. It is important that you always be alert for a pickup when the worm is sinking. Try to keep a tight line while the worm goes down, and watch your line carefully. Any twitch can mean that a bass has engulfed the worm.

Worms are usually rigged weedlessly, either by using weedless hooks or by using a Texas rig. I prefer the weedless hooks, but most bass pros and experts go with the Texas rig. Actually, it's better to avoid any weedless rig with worms unless you are fishing in weeds or heavy cover. It's difficult enough to set the hook on a weedless rig

Small plastic worms can be deadly on bass.

even with a very stiff worm rod, much less a limber fly rod.

In addition to worms, soft plastic lures have been made in the likeness of every sort of critter that bass eat, or might eat. The Creme catalog, for example, lists everything from crayfish to Wooly Worms. And the new Mister Twister curly tails and dozens of imitations are terrific for bass, and they are now available in small sizes.

My objection to soft plastic lures is that they are too soft and either tear off the hook or don't stay on it straight. And the trend at present is toward even more supersoft worms. Some bassmen take sackfuls out fishing, which is fine if you own a worm factory.

Pork lures. All the pork-rind baits I've seen will catch lots of bass either when used as a trailer, when used in connection with a spinner, or when merely put on a hook of suitable size. A 2-inch fly strip behind a spinner can be deadly.

The 4-inch bass strips, small frogs, and splittails, as well as other pork lures, are great when fished with a small hook, especially around weeds and lily pads. But I'm partial to pork eels, simply because bass, and especially the largemouth, feed extensively on eel-like creatures. A 6-inch black eel is in my opinion one of the greatest bass catchers of all time, but it is too heavy for casting with a fly rod. Much of the weight can be removed by cutting off a good part of the belly, leaving a head and the tough, but supple, rind on top.

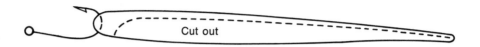

Pork eel.

I cut them down pretty much as shown in the accompanying sketch.

Bass will usually hold onto pork for some time, and, consequently, it is best to let the bass "run" a bit before setting the hook. My policy is to lower the rod tip as soon as I feel a bump or pickup, then take up the slack line and set the hook. With short lures, such as pork frogs, however, I'll strike back immediately.

Spoons. It is possible to use tiny spoons with a fly rod, and they will catch bass, with or without a trailer. But spoons are awfully heavy for their size, whereas the fly-rodder is usually, but not always, looking for large, light lures.

I make my own ultralight spoonlike metal lures from the tops of one-pound cans of Sir Walter Raleigh pipe tobacco. Similar lures, designed for bluegills, were described some time ago by John Weiss in a magazine article, and I owe the idea entirely to that article. Since the article appeared, comparable lures have been put on the market by Fin, but, again, they are designed for bluegills and aren't quite large enough for bass. The lures that Mr. Weiss described are made by cutting a circular piece of light aluminum, folding it over around a slightly undersized hook, and clamping it tight with pliers. The undersized hook is most desirable because it binds the hook's shank in the "spoon." The body of the lure acts like a keel, and the point rides up. The only difference in my bass lures is that I cut them slightly oval in shape, so that the finished lure looks more like a shad.

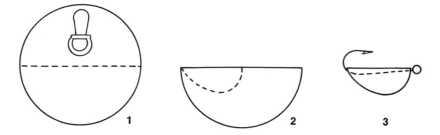

1. Remove light aluminum top from can and fold it in half. 2. Using shears or heavy scissors, cut out spoon body to desired length and shape. 3. Insert hook and clamp sides of spoon tight with pliers. Using a slightly undersized hook will help prevent the body from turning on the hook's shank. Note that the body of the spoon acts like a keel, so that the hook's point rides up.

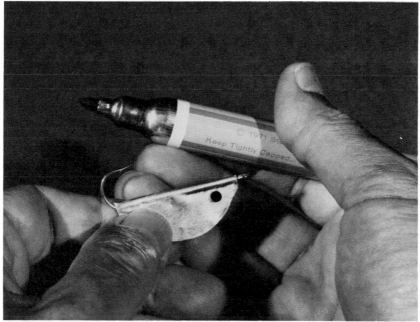

The author uses a permanent felt-tip marker to put eyes on his homemade spoons.

These lures will catch bass by being cast out and worked back in, as when one is casting to the edge of a weed bed. They'll flutter down, and can be thought of as slow-fall baits. Be alert for a pickup as the lure drops down, for a bass won't hold these things long. In my opinion, however, the major application of these lures in bass fishing is when you are casting into schooling bass. Indeed, that is why I started experimenting with them in the first place. Since other lures can be used for schooling bass, however, I prefer to discuss the technique below under a new heading.

Matching the school. Normally, bass aren't choosy about what they eat. Sometimes an exception occurs when bass are feeding on schooling shad and other baitfish. I've seen times when acres of bass have been frothing the surface all around frustrated anglers who were casting everything in their tackle boxes without a strike. Apparently the bass are so intent on catching whatever they are feeding on that they just don't see anything else. Although schooling bass will sometimes hit just about anything, the angler will usually do well to match the school not only in color and shape but also in size—exactly.

A good stock of streamers and bucktails will usually provide *something* the bass will hit, but I normally use the ultralight spoons which I have discussed already. These can be made on the spot, so if I'm after schoolers I take shears, hooks, and sheet aluminum out with me. You can try various sizes, possibly with different sizes of droppers. If you look around in the water, however, you can usually find a maimed shad on the surface, and chances are good that it will be representative of the whole school of baitfish. You can also find baitfish in the gullet of a bass taken out of the school, but you've got to catch one first.

The retrieve can also be important. The minnows are frantic when bass start tearing into the school, and, consequently, a fast retrieve works best. In fact, I fish a school by casting out and then starting the pickup for the backcast as soon as the lure touches down. Using this technique, I think, makes the fly rod ideal for schoolers. Note that a lure used on spinning or baitcasting gear has to be retrieved all the way to the boat before it can be recast into the action, whereas the fly-rodder can pick up and recast without a lengthy retrieve. It's my opinion that the fly rod has untapped potential for jump fishing.

The trouble is that most of the bass caught on the surface of a school will be small. Larger bass will sometimes lie suspended under the action, however, and can be caught by letting the lure sink down to them. Apparently the larger bass aren't as agile as the yearlings, or don't feel as frisky, and don't do as much chasing. Instead, they lie in wait for maimed baitfish to fall down. Those ultralight aluminum spoons will flutter down just right. Try them the next time you rig up for jump fishing. (For schooling seasons and related information, see Chapter 12.)

Droppers. Some fly-rodders are fond of using one or more dropper flies attached to the leader. Special leaders can be purchased with built-in dropper loops, or the angler can tie a dropper loop or two into his leader. The best bet, however, is to tie an extended blood knot in the leader. If you tie your own leaders, such a knot can be made when you are joining two sections of the leader. Proceed as you would with a regular blood knot but have enough monofilament to tie the knot with one end extending about 6 or 8 inches. (The other end can be clipped right at the knot.) Then tie a tippet onto the drop line with another blood knot.

Frankly, I think that the bass angler will do well to forget about droppers and concentrate on casting one lure accurately. When you are fishing visible cover and shorelines, accuracy is of utmost importance, and a dropper tied 3 feet from the end fly isn't going to get in close enough to the cover. Droppers cause tangles, complicate things in general, and just don't pay off in the long run.

The main application of droppers is for casting in open water, and especially into schooling bass. The action on schoolers can be fast and furious for a short time, so that the more lures you have in the water, the better your chances of connecting. Occasionally you can hook two bass on one cast—but I personally have enough trouble landing one fish at a time!

7

Going Down

ALTHOUGH THE FLY ROD is not ideal for general deepwater fishing, it does have one application that cannot be easily duplicated with either baitcasting or spinning gear. I call it snaking. The trick is to use a fast-sinking line, a fairly short leader, and a floating or slow-sinking lure. Deer-hair bugs and muddlers are ideal, but cork, balsa, and plastic bugs will also work provided that they aren't too buoyant for the line. When a cast is made over submerged brush, creek channels, and other likely bass haunts, the fast-sinking line settles to the bottom and snakes over the structure on the retrieve. The lure follows behind the line and slightly higher. Thus, the lure gets very near the structure, but not into it enough to hang frequently.

A slow, steady retrieve will work, and so will a start/stop or twitching retrieve. The lure can be worked by stripping in line or by manipulating the rod tip, but remember that raising the rod very much or stripping in a lot of line fast will cause the lure to dip downward if you have quite a lot of line out.

How high the lure runs over the line will depend on the particular lure, the length of the leader, and the rate of retrieve. If you're interested in this type of fishing, experiment in clear water.

As I said, it's best to use a short leader when you fish with a floating lure and a fast-sinking line. It is also desirable, when fishing deep, to use a short leader with regular sinking flies. If you use a 10-foot leader, you will likely have a considerable belly in your line while the lure goes down; such a belly will make it difficult to detect a strike and to set the hook. A belly can be caused either by an unweighted fly sinking slower than the line or by a weighted fly sinking faster than the line. The ideal situation is for the fly to sink at the same rate as the line.

If you've got a good fast-sinking line, almost any fly or bug can be used in deep water, but something that sinks pretty fast works better unless you want to use the sinking-line/floating-lure technique. Consider:

Weighted flies. Wet flies, streamers, and bucktails can be weighted with lead wire, but they are difficult to find in most retail outlets. Some of the mail-order houses listed in the Appendix market a few weighted flies and streamers, and any good custom craftsman can

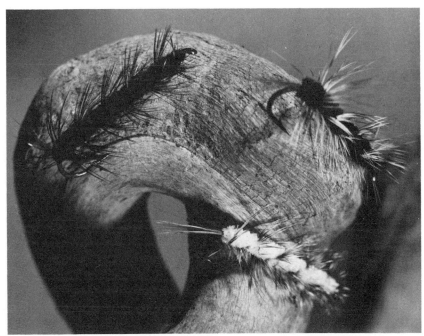

Large weighted Wooly Worms by Dan Bailey.

weight them for you. If you tie your own, remember that it's best to wrap the lead around the hook shank. The lead should be covered with lacquer, however, before you apply hair, feathers, or body materials. The reason is that the lead can discolor the pretty dressings.

Being relatively weedless, weighted keel flies are good choices when you are dredging the bottom or fishing deep in thick structure.

A streamer or bucktail can also be weighted at the head, and this gives it an up-and-down, hopping motion on the retrieve. A similar retrieve can be achieved by pinching a small piece of split shot just above the hook's eyelet.

Weighted flies work nicely with spinner attachments and pork trailers.

Jigs. Small jigs as light as ⅟₃₂ or even ⅟₆₄ ounce are available and these can be cast with a fly rod; but I don't think it's a good idea to try to cast jigs weighing ⅛ ounce and up, unless you wear a hard hat. Being heavy and virtually nonwind-resistant as compared to a large hair bug, they travel at high speed on the cast, and I've had them hit the boat almost as hard as a rifle bullet.

Although tiny jigs dressed with marabou and other stuff will certainly catch bass, and can be deadly on even trophy smallmouth, I personally prefer to add a long, thin strip of balloon rubber or some

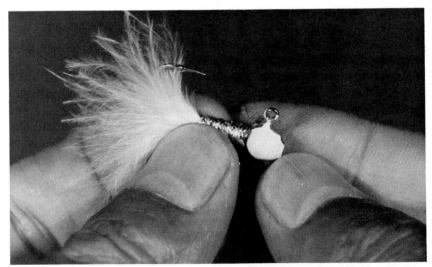

Although tiny jigs are heavy for their size, they can at times be deadly on lunker smallmouth and spotted bass.

such trailer. Often a trailer of this sort is effective on a bare jig head, without dressing. Pork strips are ideal, except that they add even more weight to a lure that is already too heavy.

Jigs will catch bass when they are fished with a slow, steady retrieve, or when they are hopped and twitched along. But by far the best bet, in my experience, is to move them up for 2 or 3 feet and let them fall back down. Most of the strikes will come while the jig is falling, so be alert. Keep a tight line and watch it carefully. Even a minute twitch can indicate that a bass has taken the lure. Sometimes, a line going slack will also indicate a strike. If in doubt, set the hook.

Another retrieve that can at times trigger a bass to strike is called ripping. The trick is to lower the rod tip, get the line tight, put both hands on the rod, and raise it above your head as fast as you can. (A fairly stiff rod is best for this retrieve.) The problem is that the bass will usually take the jig while it is falling back down, and the fly-rodder will have trouble getting the slack out of his line. An automatic reel will help.

Also try a small doglegged spinner attachment to a jig when you are ripping. The spinner blade will make a sonic disturbance that may attract bass from some distance away. A jig spinner can also be used on other retrieves.

Plastic and pork. All the soft plastic and pork lures are good choices for fishing deep. It is difficult to fish them wrong provided that you get them down close to the bass. But this doesn't mean that one retrieve is always as good as another. Day in and day out, the best method is to raise the rod tip up over your head, then tight-line the lure back down. Most of the strikes will come when the lure is falling, so be ready. Often, however, a bass will hold onto a soft plastic or pork lure, so quickness in setting the hook isn't as critical as it is with jigs and other lures. Still, you ought to know when you're getting a bite.

Diving plugs. Forget them, unless you plan to troll.

There is a practical limit to the depth one can fish by casting. If the structure or whatever you want to fish is 40 feet down and you make a 50-foot cast, your lure will be almost under the boat before it touches down. Your effective retrieve would be very short. In my opinion, it is not advisable to cast to structure deeper than 25 feet. At least not with a fly rod, except possibly with a lead shooting head and monofilament running line.

The easiest way to fish very deep water with a fly rod is to yo-yo. Or troll.

In yo-yoing, or deepwater doodlesocking, the lure is simply lowered into the water to a suitable depth, then worked up and down. The technique can be very, very effective in submerged timber, and, in fact, it is the only practical way to fish some submerged stands of timber. In one sense, the fly rod, with its long reach, is more suitable than the casting rod for yo-yoing, but the fly reel leaves much to be desired, especially for fishing in very deep water. With either spinning or free-spooling casting reels, the weight of the heavy lure will take it down, whereas with a fly reel the angler has to strip the line off by hand. In any case, yo-yoing with a fly rod works best with the heavy lures used with baitcasting or spinning rods, and "jig" spoons such as the Hopkins are favorites among bassmen.

If you fish very far out from the shoreline or very far away from visible cover, it's usually best to let your lure sink to the bottom. These anglers are fishing in Maine, a very good smallmouth state.

The strike will usually occur when the lure is falling. Set the hook immediately, and set it hard if you are using a large lure with a heavy hook. I might add that yo-yoing in thick stuff requires a heavy tippet—15- or 20-pound test.

I've never been too fond of trolling for bass even with a spinning or baitcasting rig, and certainly not with a fly rod. If you do want to troll in deep water from time to time, maybe while taking a rest from casting, it's best to use a very fast-sinking line, preferably with a lead core. A regular fly line is rather large in diameter, and tends to rise if the angler is trolling at any speed. The lead-core lines have a much smaller diameter.

I prefer weighted flies with spinners and pork attachments for trolling, and I pump my rod quite a bit instead of merely dragging the lure through the water. It's also effective to use the floating-lure/sinking-line technique, as discussed at the beginning of this chapter, but you'll have to troll very slowly. If there's a good breeze blowing in the direction you want to fish, just drift.

Also try soft plastic worms trolled very slowly, lifting the rod high from time to time and letting the worm sink down. Note that if you have too much line out, a lift of the rod will merely scoot the worm along instead of lifting it substantially.

Remember that about 90 percent of a typical lake or impoundment will be almost bassless, and merely dragging a fly across the lake randomly, without regard to water depth and submerged structure, is pretty much a waste of time. It would be more productive, for example, to troll back and forth over submerged points or islands instead of setting a straight course across the lake. (Likely spots for bass are discussed at length in Part Three.) And when you catch a bass, drop anchor or throw out a marker immediately so that you can fish the spot thoroughly. When you find one bass, there may be others around. Why troll away from them?

8

Fishing
in
Heavy Cover

MOST FLY-RODDERS WHO GO after bass like to cast around the edge of weeds, grass, lily pads, and similar cover, but they hesitate to venture a bug into the hay or into a partly submerged treetop. It is, of course, more difficult to fish in thick stuff and it is harder to get a bass out of it once you hook one, but the complete bassman will be prepared to go into the "woods" if he can't raise any action along the edges.

One very good reason for casting on into the grass (or lily pads) instead of merely to the edge of the bed is that during the retrieve the bug or fly will shake the stems underneath the water. Bass, I'm sure, can sense this movement, and, thinking it's a frog or something, may well come up to investigate. Weed shaking is especially effective if the bass are actively feeding instead of merely lazing deep in the shade. I believe so strongly in weed shaking that I'll cast into stuff so thick that the bug or fly won't even touch water, but will crawl through the tops like a squirrel. The object is to get the bass's attention and draw it out of the weeds to the open water, but I've had 8-pounders come completely out of the water after lures that hadn't even gotten wet.

One of the most suspense-packed moments in bass fishing occurs when you are working a bug in grass and suddenly see the stems parting a few yards away as a lunker homes in fast. When this happens, it is best, in my opinion, to keep the lure coming with the same retrieve. If the bass hasn't hit by the time the bug reaches open water, let it rest for a few seconds. If this happens when you're fishing with a streamer or some other sinking lure, let it sink down at the edge of the grass. With a sputterbuzzer, however, I think it's best to keep it coming even in open water. But there are other opinions on this matter.

Most bassmen fish a weed bed or similar cover with the aid of a boat and a foot-controlled, bow-mounted electric motor. The technique is to move the boat parallel to the weed bed and out about

Weedless or semiweedless lures are needed in such spots as this. These anglers are after largemouth in Georgia's Banks Lake.

30 feet from it. Thus, the angler who makes a 40- or 50-foot cast will be fishing partly in the weeds and partly in open water. I prefer this technique, but sometimes it just won't produce many bass, in which case the angler shouldn't hesitate to head the boat on into the weeds if the bed is large or wide. A good electric motor will pull a boat through surprisingly thick vegetation if the propeller is protected by a ventilated weed guard. It also helps to get the outboard out of the water, or tilted considerably.

Although a weed guard will cut down on an electric motor's efficiency, it's still a good idea to put one on even if you don't plan to enter vegetation. More than once I've been skirting weed beds and have had to use the electric to move the boat back to a lunker bass that couldn't be worked out into open water. I hesitate to give anyone advice on what to do when they tie into a real lunker in heavy cover. Personally, I head the boat toward the fish and, at the same time, try to work the fish toward me. You simply can't play a fish out under such conditions; if it stitches line through the grass, or wraps the line around a couple of thick lily-pad stems, it'll break off. However you decide to handle such a situation, you'll improve your chances of landing a lunker if you use heavy tippets in thick cover. And inspect your leader frequently for wind knots and abrasion. Some types of grass will quickly ruin a monofilament line.

One very good way to fish a grass bed is to wade, if the water isn't too deep. Wading gives the angler a lower profile than he has on most boats, and he can therefore stalk better. But he should step softly lest bass sense the vibrations. Anyone who plans to do much wade-fishing in weeds, however, will do well to cultivate a high backcast, for obvious reasons.

Any nonweedless bug or fly can be used in sparse vegetation if the angler casts it accurately and coaxes it during the retrieve. The trick is to move it gently over lily pads or through patches of grass. One good reason for sticking with nonweedless lures as long as possible is that, strike for strike, they'll hook more bass than weedless lures. But, of course, weedless bugs are necessary in really thick stuff.

Regardless of lure, the direction of the retrieve can be important in avoiding snags in vegetation and in such cover as submerged treetops. Grass stems will often be leaning in one direction, according to the wind and wave action, and the angler can avoid some snags by retrieving in the direction of the bend instead of across the stems. In lily pads, it's always wise to maneuver line and lure to avoid those troublesome crotches where the pad joins the stem. In fallen treetops, it's best to retrieve parallel to the limbs instead of across them; further, retrieving a lure from the trunk end toward the tips of the limbs can avoid some severe hang-ups in forks.

Deer-hair frogs and mice can be tied so that the hair on the body covers the point of the hook. Some other hair patterns, such as the Henshall bugs, can be tied with a hair "beard" that serves as a weed guard. These hair lures are not ultraweedless, and should therefore be worked very gently when the going gets thick.

Arbogast, Weber, and other firms market weedless cork and plastic bugs for fishing in thick stuff. Typically, these have a wire weed guard that works much like the guards on weedless worm hooks. I find that such guards are usually too stiff, thereby causing the angler to miss too many strikes. I nearly always weaken the wire by depressing it severely and letting it spring back up.

A weedless hair moth tied by Poul Jorgensen. Note that the body hair is trimmed so that a beard protects the point of the hook.

To make a cork or balsa bug weedless, cut a piece of leader wire and bend it to resemble a hairpin. Insert both ends of the wire through the bug, working from top to bottom. The wire should pass on either side of the hook's shank.

Although a number of weedless bugs are on the market, it is sometimes difficult to find them in local tackle shops. In a pinch, almost any cork or balsa bug can be made weedless with a few inches of light leader wire. The first step is to bend the wire with needle-nosed pliers or form it around a nail partly driven into a flat surface. The formed wire should resemble a hairpin, but the sides should be closer together. Push the two ends of the wire through the bug's body, one end on either side of the hook's shank. Pull the wire down tightly on top of the bug's body. Then bend the two bottom ends back to form guards for either side of the hook's point. The accompanying photographs should clear up any questions.

Some bugs are semiweedless without any additional weed guards. The hackle "wings" on most poppers and similar cork, balsa, and plastic bugs can be tied so that they more or less protect the point of the hook. This semi-weedless design works best on the slider-type bugs; the bullet shape of the bug's nose permits it to be worked out of tight spots without much resistance.

After the wire has been inserted and snugged down, turn the bug over and bend the ends back toward the hook. Trim the ends to approximately the length indicated in this photograph.

Pork eels and frogs, as well as small worms and other soft plastic lures, can be put onto weedless hooks, and, when properly rigged, are the most snag-free of all lures. They are also very productive when fished in weeds and pads because they resemble snakes, leeches, and so on.

I often fish such lures rather fast in thick stuff, then let them sink in potholes or at the edge of the weed bed. The idea is to draw the bass out into open water before it takes the lure—but often a fast retrieve brings a strike in the hay. I've had bass hit at such lures three or four times on a single retrieve in very thick lily pads and in grass. Such a fast retrieve can be quite effective at times, usually in the warmer months when snakes and other animals, as well as bass, are more active. I've even used an automatic reel to zip pork eels along.

But don't rely on fast retrieves. A slowly worked lure will usually be more effective, and don't hesitate to let a worm or eel lie still for a minute, either on the bottom or atop a lily pad.

Although soft plastic and pork lures are great bass catchers, those
of any size are too heavy for easy casting with a fly rod. It is possible to tie streamers and bucktails on weedless worm hooks, but as
far as I know such flies are not widely available. Streamers and bucktails tied on the new keel hooks, however, are coming on strong. Because of the weight distribution in the shank, the point of a keel hook
rides up, and the wings of the streamer or bucktail help protect the
point of the hook. I feel that flies tied on keel hooks have great potential for bass fishing in vegetation and heavy cover of all sorts. I
would like to see some good firm market long, sparsely dressed bucktails designed to imitate eels and sirens instead of minnows. Keel
hooks might also have potential in deer-hair surface bugs. In fact,
Keel Fly Company markets a muddlerlike surface lure called Miracle
Bug, and it comes through grass and brush nicely.

*Bugs and flies tied on keel hooks are great for fishing in weeds and thick
cover.*

I do, however, have reservations about the hooking power, or "bite," of the keel design. On the other hand, it is difficult to set hooks that have wire guards, and keel hooks could turn out to be the better choice. In any case, keel streamers and bucktails are the only sensible choice for tying weedless bass "flies." The combination of light weight for casting and weedlessness for fishing will, I think, open up a whole new ball game for fly-rodders who go after bass. I've already seen reports of several 8- and 9-pound largemouth being taken on keel flies fished in the expansive grass beds of Florida lakes.

There is one unorthodox application of the fly rod for fishing deep in thick weeds, lily pads, submerged timber, and so on. I'm talking about vertical jigging, or doodlesocking. The trick is to lower a heavy lure to the bottom and jiggle it up and down. The technique has

Any lure that sputters on the surface during a fast retrieve can be deadly on bass in weeds and lily pads.

caught tons of bass, and it is really the best way to present a lure to bass that are deep down in impossible cover. The longer and stiffer the rod, the better it works for doodlesocking. Since no casting is required, spoons, jigs, and other heavy, fast-sinking lures can be used.

I admit that I've done a little doodlesocking when no one was looking and when all else had failed to get a rise, but I can't really recommend using a fly rod in this rude manner, especially when a cane pole will work better. But fly-rodders don't usually tote cane poles around with them, and it might be a good idea to hide a heavy jig in your fly box, just in case the need arises. Anyone guilty of habitual doodlesocking with a fine fly stick, however, ought to have his name struck from the Orvis mailing list, and surely ought to be forever banned from the Brotherhood of the Jungle Cock.

Part Three

When and Where
to
Catch Bass

MORE THAN ONCE I'VE HEARD and read that bass are where you find them. True. And you'll usually find them in some sort of cover or around some sort of submerged structure. There are exceptions, and numbers of bass have been caught in open water. Nonetheless, the bass angler will greatly improve his chances by keeping his bug, fly, or lure close to either visible cover or submerged structure.

The term "structure" is rather broad, and, frankly, I dislike the word. But it is now so widely established among bass anglers that it would be foolish to try to communicate with another such term. (The same can be said for "migration route," a term which isn't truly accurate but which communicates nonetheless.) Anyhow, structure can be defined as any irregularity in the lake or impoundment bottom, such as a creek channel, a submerged roadbed, or an underwater ledge. The term "substructure" designates an irregularity in the structure, such as an island or a high point in a submerged creek channel.

Anyhow, the secret of successful bass fishing boils down to locating the fish and then knowing how to catch them. Knowing something about the ways and habits of black bass will help, but it is equally important to learn the particular lake or impoundment you plan to fish. In theory, the longer you fish a piece of water, the more bass you should be able to catch out of it. But this does not mean that success can't be quick. The modern bassman, with his depth finders and topographic maps, can learn more about a lake in three days than some anglers would discover in a lifetime. I might add, however, that merely having a $6,000 bass boat fully rigged with all manner of electronic devices won't make an expert bassman out of a poor fisherman, just as a $200 fly rod won't necessarily make an expert caster out of an angler who doesn't know how to use it.

9

The Basses and Their Habitat

WHEN I WAS A BOY not much taller than my stack of fishing magazines, I used to read about black bass and wish that we had some in our neck of the woods. We did. We had lots of them. Only we called them trout, and I still hear them called trout, or green trout, from time to time. Actually, I had caught numbers of bass on the local streams and lakes, and no doubt had taken even redeyes and spots. Even today many anglers think only in terms of largemouth and smallmouth, and possibly spotted bass. There are, however, at least 11 species or subspecies of bass.

The perennial argument over which bass is the better fighter, pound for pound, is in my opinion quite ridiculous. There is far too much difference between one individual bass and another within each species, and far too much depends on where a bass is caught, how it is hooked, how cold or warm the water is, and so on.

There are also some myths along this line. Some anglers believe that a bass caught in cold water will "pull better" and fight harder than a bass from warmer water. This simply isn't true. I've caught bass in water so cold that they pulled hardly at all. (I've also caught bass in water so warm that it apparently made them sluggish.) My experience indicates that bass caught in deep, clear lakes pull better than those caught in shallow, murky water, possibly because they are healthier; but this is merely my opinion, and other anglers may well disagree. One thing that is certain is that any healthy bass caught from a clean stream pulls better than one caught from a lake. As Jason Lucas put it, even an old shoe puts up a pretty good fight in current! Another point that is pretty certain is that a bass, regardless of species, caught in shallow water is more likely to jump than one caught in deep water.

I do, however, have a definite opinion on which is the better bass for the *fly-rodder*. It's neither the largemouth nor the smallmouth. It's a little redeye, a relatively unimportant species that I will discuss in due course. The order of the bass in the following breakdown is based not on my personal preference but on the importance of the species in terms of availability on a nationwide basis:

Largemouth bass (*Micropterus salmoides*). The largemouth bass is the biggest of all the black basses, and the species now ranges in all of the mainland states as well as in parts of Southern Canada, Mexico, Cuba, and Central America. It has also been stocked in Africa, Japan, and other places around the globe. The largemouth is by far more adaptable than the other basses and most other game fish, which makes it a very good candidate for stocking in any impoundment across the country. The largemouth's original range included the Mississippi and the Ohio River systems, all the way from the Gulf of Mexico on up into Canada; it extended east to Florida and north up the Atlantic to Maryland.

An important subspecies, the Florida largemouth, attains a weight of over 20 pounds. (In the northern states, however, regular largemouth seldom exceed 10 or 12 pounds.) The original range of this bass included only peninsula Florida, southern Georgia, and possibly southeastern Alabama. Recently, however, the Florida largemouth has been stocked in California, Texas, and other states.

As a general rule, largemouth show a marked preference for grass beds and other forms of vegetation. They will go deep—and I've caught 8-pounders at 35 feet—but they don't usually go as deep as the smallmouth and the spotted bass. Because the largemouth is more likely, day in and day out, to hit on or near the surface, I'd have to rate it a tad above the smallmouth as a fly-rod fish. But a lot of anglers, and especially those who fish for smallmouth in streams, will take issue with that statement, and rather hotly so.

As shown in the accompanying drawings, the largemouth is easily distinguished from the smallmouth and the other basses because its jaw juts back behind the eye. Also, the largemouth's dorsal fin has more of a gap between the spiny- and soft-ray portions.

Largemouth are primarily lake fish, whereas smallmouth are primarily stream fish. It is therefore somewhat ironic that the world's record smallmouth (11 pounds 15 ounces) came from TVA's Dale Hollow Lake, and the world's record largemouth (22 pounds 4 ounces) came from a wide spot, known as "Lake Montgomery," in Georgia's Ocmulgee River! Anyhow, largemouth do well in some rivers as well as in some brackish-water areas.

Popping bugs are probably the best fly-rod lures for largemouth, provided that the bass are feeding on top. But the largemouth will hit anything that moves in, on, or over the water. Generally, they prefer larger lures than do the smallmouth or the spotted bass—but I've seen 10-pounders that went for 1-inch lures.

Largemouth bass

1. Upper jaw extends beyond eye.
2. Usually broad black stripe.
3. Separation between soft and spiny dorsal fins.

Smallmouth bass

1. Upper jaw does not extend beyond eye.
2. Vertical bars on sides.
3. Not as much separation between soft and spiny dorsal fins.

This nice largemouth was caught in North Carolina. On bass this size, the dark stripe along the lateral line fades out.

Smallmouth bass (*Micropterus dolomieui*). As shown in the drawings on page 101, the smallmouth is easily distinguished from the largemouth because its jaw does not jut back past the eye and because its dorsal fin doesn't have as much of a gap between the spiny- and soft-ray portions. The smallmouth doesn't have teeth on its tongue as the spotted bass has, and it doesn't have the reddish eye and fins of the redeye.

Apparently, the smallmouth's original range was rather restricted, located principally in the Ohio River drainage systems. But in the latter 1800s it was transplanted to many states via the railroads. It is still primarily a northern bass, although the world's record breakers have come from Tennessee, Kentucky, and North Alabama. Several attempts have been made to stock the fish in Florida, but with little success. The bass will live in some of the Florida streams, but will not reproduce in them. The smallmouth has apparently been stocked successfully in some of the colder Texas impoundments, but how well it does there over the long run remains to be seen. A subspecies, the

Neosho smallmouth, grows in the swift waters of the Neosho River and some tributaries of the Arkansas River in the Ozarks. Recent impoundments have pretty much restricted the Neosho's habitat to the upper reaches of tributary streams. The Neosho is a little longer than the regular smallmouth, and can be identified by its lower jaw, which juts out far enough to expose its teeth.

Although the regular smallmouth is primarily a stream fish, it does quite well in cool, clear, rocky impoundments and lakes that are at least 25 feet deep. In general, the smallmouth stays a little deeper than the largemouth and doesn't feed quite as much on the surface. But bugs and surface lures will catch smallmouth—and lots of them, especially in suitable streams. In either streams or impoundments, smallmouth are fond of rock structure.

Smallmouth will sometimes show a marked preference for small

A Pennsylvania smallmouth.

lures, and at least in this respect they are a better fish than the large-mouth for being taken on light fly rods and on ultralight spinning rigs. Smallmouth are also more likely to take dry flies, and probably feed more extensively on insects. I also feel that smallmouth in general feed more extensively on crayfish, but of course a good deal depends on what food is available. They will eat just about anything in the water, and will sometimes gorge themselves, but in general they are not quite as gluttonous as largemouth.

In impoundments, smallmouth tend to go a little too deep for ideal fly-rodding, but on most days they will move in to the shoreline or to shallow structure early in the morning and late in the afternoon, as well as at night. Early morning and late afternoon are also best on streams, but as a rule a good stream will offer better midday fly-rodding than an impoundment will. Often, the only way to get action on impoundments is to go deep with jigs, jig-and-eel combinations, and similar bottom bumpers.

As a rule, one has a better chance of catching trophy smallmouth in the impoundments in North Alabama, Tennessee, and Kentucky, but excellent smallmouth fishing can be found from Oregon to Maine, as well as in Canada and even Newfoundland.

Spotted bass (*Micropterus punctulatus*). Sometimes called the Kentucky bass, spots seem to be a hybrid between the largemouth and the smallmouth. The distinguishing spots occur in lengthwise rows below the lateral line and are formed by scales that have dark bases. The spotted bass also has teeth on its tongue, which separates it from the smallmouth and largemouth bass, but not necessarily from the Suwannee bass or the Guadalupe bass.

The spotted bass ranges from northwest Florida westward to Texas, Oklahoma, and Kansas, and throughout the Ohio and the Mississippi River systems. In some impoundments, spots outnumber the other basses; in Georgia's Lake Allatoona, for example, from 60 to 80 percent of the black bass caught are spots. Alabama's Lake Lewis Smith is generally considered to be one of the very best lakes for spots, and the world's record, 8 pounds 10½ ounces, came from that impoundment.

There are two subspecies. The Alabama spotted bass grows in the Alabama River system, which extends westward into Mississippi via the Tombigbee River and eastward into Georgia via the Coosa and the Tallapoosa. The other subspecies, the Wichita spotted bass, grows in the streams of the Wichita mountains in Oklahoma.

On most of the impoundments, spots prefer deep water—up to 100 feet—along steep, rocky banks and bluffs. In my experience, spots in streams also show a marked preference for rocky bottom or structure.

Because spots are often in deep water, they are not the ideal fish for the fly rod, especially in some of the deep, clear impoundments. They can, however, be caught on tiny jigs and similar lures. Spots *will* hit on, or near, the surface when they are in shallow water, and some streams do provide excellent spot fishing for the fly-rodder.

Redeye bass (*Micropterus coosae*). Also called shoal bass, Flint River smallmouth, Chipola bass, and no doubt other names, the redeye is a stream fish and will not reproduce in ponds and lakes. It prefers stretches of rocky, fairly swift streams. The redeye's range is rather limited, as compared to the largemouth, the smallmouth, and even the spotted bass. According to *McClane's New Standard Fishing Encyclopedia*, the redeye is found in the Alabama, the Coosa, and the Tallapoosa River systems in Alabama, the Chattahoochee and the Flint River systems in Georgia, the Conasauga drainage in southeastern Tennessee, and the Chipola River in Florida. I've also caught them in the Choctawhatchee River in southeastern Alabama. Recently, redeye bass have been transplanted to Texas and possibly other states.

Actually, there are at least two forms of this bass: the Alabama redeye and the Apalachicola River redeye (or Georgia redeye). The Alabama form grows larger, and the currently accepted world's record (6 pounds ½ ounce) was caught in Hallawakee Creek, Alabama. Generally, the redeye looks like a smallmouth, but can be identified easily by the red color of its eyes; the anal, caudal, and dorsal fins are also red. The Alabama form is usually of a brighter color than the Apalachicola form, but the Apalachicola form usually has a more pronounced basicaudal spot (which may not even be visible on the Alabama form). I've heard, and read, that redeyes grow up to 8 pounds in Georgia's Flint River, but there is some disagreement, and dispute, about these "Flint River smallmouth." Anyhow, the average size of the redeye is about a pound.

The redeye feeds more extensively on insects than the other basses do. In fact, a good part of its food is taken by surface feeding, and this should be enough to perk up a fly-rodder's interest. Small bugs will usually produce, but the angler should also take along a few streamers and spinners in case the bass are in deeper pools. The red-

These redeye bass were taken in northwest Florida's Chipola River, where they are called Chipola bass. The redeye is a great fly-rod fish because it feeds extensively on insects.

eye puts up a good fight for its size and is noted for its jumping and headshaking tactics. Anyhow, a biologist has called the redeye the brook trout of warm-water species, and I say that pound for pound the redeye has to be the fly-rodder's choice.

Guadalupe bass (*Micropterus treculi*). This small bass, which seldom exceeds 12 inches in length, was until recently believed to be a subspecies of the spotted bass. Now some biologists believe it to be a separate species, and *McClane's* treats it as a separate species. Anyhow, it is native to the spring-fed streams of Central Texas, such as the Pedernales, Colorado, and Guadalupe rivers. It does live in associated impoundments, but it is primarily a stream fish and shows a preference for swift water in shoals and riffles.

Positive identification is difficult. The Guadalupe closely resembles the spotted bass, but it is a little more spotted. On some specimens the spots occur both above and below the lateral line, whereas on spotted bass they occur only below the lateral line. The Guadalupe has teeth on its tongue (as does the spot). The Guadalupe has 8 to 9 scale rows above the lateral line, 15 to 17 below. (These figures are from *McClane's*; other sources list 7 to 10 above, 14 to 19 below.)

The Guadalupe will take small poppers and other surface lures, but streamers, sparse bucktails, small spoons, and other minnow imitations are probably better. Spinner-streamer combinations are also good.

Suwannee bass (*Micropterus notius*). Like the Guadalupe bass, the Suwannee is a separate species that seldom grows longer than 12 inches. This small bass has characteristics of the redeye and the spotted basses. Its distinguishing mark, however, is the bright blue (bluish-green, or turquoise) color on its lower belly and chin. The Suwannee's range is limited to the tannic waters of Florida's Suwannee River and its tributaries. I have heard reports of this bass being in the Ochlockonee River in northwest Florida, but they are certainly not common in this river.

One almost unique point about the Suwannee bass is that it usually stays in midstream instead of hanging out around stumps and logs and undercuts in the bank. Also, the fish seems to feed primarily on crayfish, and therefore doesn't hit surface bugs as readily as the redeye does.

The bass can be taken on any part of the Suwannee River system, all the way to within a mile or so of the Gulf of Mexico. But the best bet is in the swift, rocky stretches of the lower Santa Fe and Ichetuckee tributaries. Remember to fish open water, preferably when the stream is low.

The black bass is considered to be one of the more intelligent freshwater game fish in the country. I'm not sure, however, that intelligence is the right word, and anyone who thinks that a bass is smarter than he is will never have enough confidence to make an expert fisherman. I think that too many anglers overrate the intelligence of bass—and underrate their senses.

Hearing. The black bass has an excellent sense of hearing, owing to sensory mechanisms along its lateral line and other parts of its body. It also has an inner ear and a related hollow bone structure that may amplify sound or vibrations. In any case, bass can detect even minute vibrations in the water from some distance away. Moreover, a bass can tell the speed and direction of the source of the vibrations. Thus, the bass can easily home in on a moving lure, or can be alerted to a lure's approach. By the same token, it can easily be spooked by anglers, and is especially wary of such noises as a paddle being banged against an aluminum boat, an angler stomping along a bank, or an anchor thrown splashing into the water and thudding down on a rock bottom.

The noise factor is probably more important in quiet, remote ponds and streams than it is on lakes that are heavily fished and constantly used by pleasure boaters. But the large bass in such a lake didn't survive by being insensitive to such blatant, unnatural sounds. In short, the wise angler will avoid all unnecessary noise, no matter where he fishes.

I may be too much of a stickler on this point, but I don't enjoy fishing with most other anglers because they make too much noise in the boat, and are continuously fussing around in their tackle boxes, banging on the bottom of the boat, clanking on this or that. It's true that I am a bit too fussy. It's also true that I catch more than my share of lunker bass. And I catch most of them when I am alone and quiet.

Smell and taste. Although the bass doesn't feed as extensively as the bullhead by olfactory senses, it is not entirely insensitive to taste and smell. A good deal of experimentation is currently going on with scented lures, and for some time now plastic-worm buffs have been using this flavor or that. Whether bass are attracted to certain flavors is, in my opinion, open to question. I am, however, certain that some smells and tastes can repel bass, and the fly-rodder will do well to keep gasoline, oil, and the serine in human perspiration off his lures and leaders. I don't think that any sort of added scent is necessary, but I do think the angler should wash his hands frequently with soap and water and keep his tackle box clean.

One related point that may be very important is that many fish and other aquatic creatures emit some sort of chemical substance when they are wounded. This substance attracts predators, but serves as a warning to others of its kind. Thus, a shiner with a hook stuck in it might attract a bass. But a bass that has been hooked or otherwise hurt can alert other bass in the area to danger. I believe this, and I seldom release a bass in the vicinity in which I caught it. This can be especially important when bass are tightly grouped around deepwater structure, and less important when they are foraging for food along the shoreline. One of the worst things you can do is break a bass off when you are fishing a "school." Some of the bass pros are noted for horsing a bass out of the water, and this tactic may be the best way not because it increases the odds on landing a particular bass but because it doesn't spook the school as much as "playing" the bass would.

Still another point is that a bass often hits a lure too quickly for its olfactory senses to warn it of any danger. But as soon as it gets the lure in its mouth, it tastes the thing and spits it out. The quicker the angler can set the hook, the better; and the angler who is always alert and expecting a strike will almost always catch more bass than one who doesn't watch his business. I believe this strongly, and I would estimate that when the average angler is fishing subsurface lures that are jigged or allowed to fall in one way or another he will detect less than half of his strikes or pickups. I've *seen* bass pick up a lure and spit it out unbeknown to the angler.

Vision. I've said more than once, both in conversation and in print, that in my opinion some of the bass boats with high seats mounted on a fishing deck are not desirable for fishing in clear, shallow water. The bass can see you. On the other hand, I've caught bass which, I'm convinced, went ahead and hit because the lure was traveling toward the boat. In other words, the bass hit in a now-or-never situation. I've even caught 7- or 8-pound bass within a few feet of the boat. But I've lost a good deal more fish than I've caught because of the presence of the boat. I've seen hundreds of bass run at a lure, see the boat, and swirl off. Or so it seemed. In any case, I firmly believe that if you are fly-rodding in shallow water from a high pedestal seat or standing up to cast, you'll do well to make longer casts. You should also avoid white or bright shirts and hats when you are fishing in shallow, clear water, but I must add that this is my own opinion and that some experts disagree.

I recently read an article by Buck Rogers in *Field & Stream* (April 1975), and it supports my belief that bass can see an angler. Mr. Rogers has some interesting things to say about a bass's vision and color perception:

Like most predators, a bass has good eyesight. Its eyes are located on either side of its head, and each of these eyes has a 180-degree field of vision. Best depth perception is dead ahead where both eyes provide binocular vision to close in on a fleeing quarry. But vision is as good at a 90-degree angle to either side, and up and down as well. How well a bass sees in its watery environment depends on the clarity of the water, the amount of sunlight overhead, and the depth of the water.

Bass can see out of their aquatic environment, too. When the surface of the water is calm they can see everything from straight up to a 20-degree angle with the water surface. At this angle, and below, light is reflected away from the water and vision is blurred. This means that a bass will not be able to see you if you are on the shore at the water's edge, of sitting in a low profile boat. If you are standing, though, or perched high on a bass-boat seat, you probably will be visible to a bass swimming a few feet beneath the water's surface.

Bass have good color perception, also. Test after test have proven that the species can differentiate between colors and are particularly responsive to such colors as red, orange, and yellow. Red, while highly visible at the surface, fades rapidly as the depth of the water increases. A bright red lure will appear almost black to bass at a depth of 10 feet or more. Yellow and white retain their color quality at extreme depths as do orange, blue, and green. The latter two colors, which are the same hue as a bass's environment, were not particularly appealing to largemouth in the color experiments conducted.

Now, what does this information mean to you? It indicates that color is significant in lures that run close to the surface of the water and less of a factor when fished deep. Exceptions to this rule are yellow, white, and silver, which retain their identity in extreme depth. Color is also more of a factor on a sunny day. In dim light, bass have more trouble identifying colors than we do, so in these cases lure color is less a factor than action and size.

The subject of color in surface lures is controversial, so I put on a diver's mask and went down on the bottom to get a bass's perspective of the subject. All I saw was a silhouette in varying shades of gray. A white lure was a distinct shadow silhouetted against the overhead sun, but when a cloud covered the sun it became less visible. Red lures appeared black, as did brown and dark green. I couldn't at any depth distinguish color in these surface lures and I quite frankly do not believe a bass can, either.

As a fish moves closer to a lure resting on the surface, and particularly if it is a few feet to the side, color becomes a little more significant. Under such circumstances a yellow darter can be distinguished from a white one. Viewed from the side and just below the water surface, color is identifiable.

All of this means that except in clear water and bright light, a fish sees the silhouette of a surface lure more than its actual color. Hence, in dim light conditions a dark surface lure, regardless of color, will be easier for a bass to see than would be a light one.

I don't believe that bass are quite as leader shy as some wild trout are, but there is no doubt that a small leader will often produce more strikes. (For one thing, a small leader isn't as stiff as a heavy one, and thereby permits better lure action.) Further, I think that some bass have sharper vision than others. The Florida largemouth, used to chasing frogs and snakes and large shiners, probably doesn't have as keen an eye as does the redeye bass, which feeds primarily on floating insects. I've seen the water literally covered with mayflies or love bugs without a single largemouth rising to them, although they were taking plastic worms fished 4 or 5 feet deep. I don't think the largemouth even saw the mayflies or love bugs, whereas redeye or smallmouth might have been frothing the water after them. Further, I believe that the smallmouth and the redeye are more leader shy than largemouth are. It could be, however, that the largemouth saw the mayflies and just didn't give a damn about them, and that they see heavy tippets and just don't give a damn about them, either! As Charles Waterman said in another context, only the fish know for sure how they see a leader, and they may well disagree among themselves.

Temper. Many anglers have claimed that the bass will sometimes hit a lure not because it wants to eat the thing but because it is angry at it, or just plain aggressive. I too believe this.

There are two approaches to making a bass mad. One is to cast repeatedly to a likely spot with a loud, fast, or outlandish lure. The other is to "play" a bug or surface plug, letting it sit dead for several seconds (or even minutes), then twitching it ever so gently, popping it, letting it sit still again, and so on, much like teasing a kitten with a string. Sometimes the bass will pounce on the lure just to make it move again.

Whatever triggers a bass's temper, I suspect that it is cocked by a territorial imperative, which is, of course, at its strongest when the bass is bedding or fanning out a bed. At this time, a bass will hit a lure just to chase it away from the bed. Other fish will also do this, and I heard of a lowly bowfin (grindle, mudfish, or whatever you call it) that jumped up on a bank after a couple of kids who were poking into a school of newly hatched bowfin fry!

A bass will also take a stand in a pocket or on the shady side of a stump and lie waiting for food to come by. Such a bass can be caught, I believe, on a lure that hasn't fooled the bass as to its edibility. What would you do, if you were a hungry bass and had taken a stand at a strategic spot while waiting for a siren or shiner to come by when, suddenly, a popping bug started making enough ruckus on the surface to scare any sensible shiner or siren away? You'd probably sit there for a while, gritting your teeth and cursing the thing. If it kept coming back, you might pack up and leave. Or you might bow up, your gills working faster, until finally you struck the thing.

In all honesty, however, I'm not at all certain that a bass will hit out of anger or frustration except when it is on the bed. Still, I am convinced that the angler will do well to believe this theory. To believe, in other words, that he can catch bass when they aren't biting. Such a philosophy will make him fish harder, and will make his fishing more of a challenge—a personal thing between man and bass.

In any case, it is a known fact that bass, and often lunkers, will hit a lure not on the first or second cast, but on the fifth or sixth. Just the other day, I was trying some new and fancy casts in my boat basin. I must have made a hundred casts near some grass just across the canal, when, suddenly, a 5-pounder hit my bug violently and came on out of the water shaking its head. The thing took me by such surprise that I didn't hook it, and probably didn't attempt to set the hook. Hell, I wasn't even fishing.

10

Seasonal and Daily Variables

THERE IS SUCH A VAST difference in seasonal changes and bass fishing from North to South and from coast to coast—and often within a single state—that any irrefutable discussion of fishing by seasons of the year would have to be either quite general or tediously long. As an extreme example, fly-rodding for bass in Florida's Lake Okeechobee can be very good in February, whereas fly-rodding on some of the bass lakes in, say, Michigan, may be impossible because of a frozen surface. (Bass can, however, be caught through the ice.)

If you are unfamiliar with a lake, impoundment, or area you plan to fish, it is best to make inquiries at local tackle shops and marinas, or to talk to expert bass anglers and professional guides, before you start fishing. Yet people, and even experts, tend to have false notions about seasonal fishing in any one area, so that local advice may not always be the best. More than one bassman from out-of-state has shown the local boys a thing or two. I fear that many opinions on seasonal bass fishing are based more on the habits and creature comforts of anglers than on those of black bass. The new crop of scientific bassmen, armed with electronic fishing aids, have proven

Early mornings and late afternoons are usually the best times to catch bass with a fly rod, especially with surface bugs. These anglers are on Guntersville Lake in Alabama.

time and again that bass can be caught winter, spring, summer, and fall, at dawn, noonday, sundown, and night.

Because a good deal depends on geographic location and on the characteristics of a particular lake or impoundment or stream, I believe that such factors as water depth, oxygen content, subsurface temperature, structure availability, and so on are the proper guides to fishing a particular lake at a particular time. These will be discussed later in this chapter. Meanwhile, a few comments on seasonal trends won't, I hope, be too far amiss:

Winter. Bass tend to go deep when the water gets cold, and they don't feed as much in shallow water even early and late during the day, or at night. The reason they go deep and stay deep is, in my opinion, that frogs, snakes, spring lizards, and so forth hibernate and there simply isn't as much food stirring about along the shoreline or in shallow-water areas. Sometimes, however, you can have a field day by fishing in very shallow water on warm, sunny winter days.

One point to remember when you are fishing in cold water is that the bass themselves slow down. They eat less food, and won't move fast or far to catch a lure. Small baits and slow, deep retrieves are therefore in order.

Summer. The so-called summer slump is a myth. Early mornings and late afternoons during the summer months are among the most productive times to fish popping bugs. During midday, however, the bass are likely to go deep, or hole up in heavy cover. Night fishing with surface lures is good in summer months, especially in lakes that are heavily used by pleasure boaters.

Fall. In most areas, fall offers excellent surface fishing. Bass often go on a shoreline feeding binge just before frogs and snakes and such things start to hibernate.

Spring. Everybody wants to go fishing on a fine spring day, and the bass too seem to be fond of getting out of their winter holes to roam about. In spring, you can often get good action all day on popping bugs and other surface lures.

Spawning season. Spawning season varies from winter to spring to summer. In Florida, I've seen bass bed as early as December. In the northern states, spawning is usually as late as June or even July.

More lunker bass are caught during the spawning season than in the rest of the year. This is especially true of lunker largemouth, which bed in very shallow water (1 to 5 feet) and often very close to the shore. There are several reasons why very large bass are so vulnerable at this time: (1) Old sow bass mill around in shallow water before selecting a bedding spot. (2) They feed heavily just before and just after spawning. (3) They will often attack anything that comes near their bed. (4) The angler can spot the beds, which are often 4 or 5 feet in diameter, and can therefore fish to the bass. I have mixed feelings about it, but I have caught some real lunkers by spotting beds. Just the other day, for example, I was fishing with a high school boy who was visiting us at our place on Florida's Lake Weir. He had a new spinning rig and wanted to catch himself some bass. We caught a few and were fishing along when, thanks to my polarized sunglasses, I saw a faint white circle on the bottom in some 5 feet of water. It seemed to have a shadow on it. The shadow moved off. Quickly I hit the foot-controlled electric motor and eased away. I told the young fellow that there was a lunker bass down there and that he could catch it if he tried hard enough. About an hour later, he did hook the bass and wrestled it out. She weighed a little over 11½ pounds!

As I said, though, I have mixed feelings about catching bass off the bed, and I seldom deliberately go out looking for beds. Smallmouth and the other species, as well as the northern largemouth, however, aren't quite as vulnerable as the Florida largemouth because they usually bed in deeper water. Smallmouth in some impoundments bed as deep as 20 feet.

Schooling time. Generally, bass school more in the summer months, but on some lakes they school in spring and fall as well as summer. In Florida, I've seen minor schooling activity in November and December.

So much for seasonal variations. On a daily basis, bass tend to stay in deepwater haunts during midday. Early in the morning and late in the afternoon, as well as at night, they are likely to feed in shallow water. Moreover, they will move from deep water to shallow, and back again, along established paths, such as submerged ditches and creek beds. When they are holding in deep water, they are likely to bunch up pretty tightly. But when they reach a shoreline or other feeding area, they will usually scatter. They will sometimes seem to school when they are feeding on baitfish, but bass are individuals and don't follow the mass mentality of, say, schools of mullet. They don't necessarily migrate from one spot to another in a pack, and there will usually be some holdover bass in feeding areas at any time of day.

There will also usually be some bass in deep haunts even during prime feeding time.

The bass pros talk a lot about establishing a pattern. It makes sense, but remember that there may be several effective patterns for the day. In one tournament, for example, one successful contestant caught his bass in 30 feet of water. Another caught his in 3 feet. So there you have it. Bass are where you find them. Before you start making random casts, however, remember that bass show marked preferences for cover and structure, as discussed in Chapter 11 and 12. Also consider the following physical variables:

Oxygen. The amount of oxygen dissolved in the water can be extremely important in bass fishing. In some cases, there won't be enough oxygen to support them. This usually happens during the hot summer months on the larger lakes, owing to thermal stratification. But decaying vegetation, which consumes oxygen, can also deplete certain areas—or whole lakes.

For most fly-rodding situations in shallow water, there will usually be enough oxygen to support bass. Even so, the action will be better in areas where the oxygen content is high. Experimentation with one of the oxygen monitors will bear this out. If you don't have an oxygen monitor, remember that wave action will certainly help oxygenate the water, the spots where waves are breaking on rocky banks or riprap may be hot. Remember also that live vegetation produces oxygen during the daylight hours through photosynthesis.

Light intensity. Because bass have fixed pupils and no eyelids, they have no way of regulating the amount of light that reaches the retina, except by going deeper into the water or seeking out shade. They can and do tolerate bright light at times, especially when they are bedding in shallow water, but generally the larger bass do seem to avoid brightness. Whether or not they are actually uncomfortable (and if so, to what degree) in bright light has not been settled to my satisfaction. My question is whether they avoid bright light because of discomfort or because they may feel safer or more secure in darker waters.

Whatever the reasons, I do feel that light intensity is very important in bass fishing. Here are some variables that have an influence on underwater light intensity:

Position of the sun. Early and late during the day, the sun's rays hit the water at a narrow angle; reflection is at a maximum, and depth of penetration is at a minimum. Reduced sunlight penetration

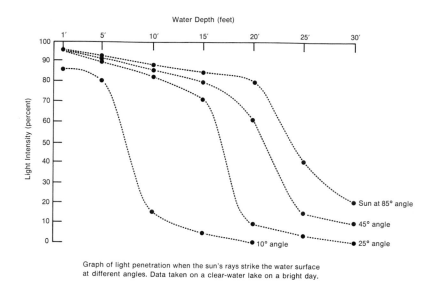

Graph of light penetration when the sun's rays strike the water surface at different angles. Data taken on a clear-water lake on a bright day.

is the reason why bass fishing in shallow water is usually better early and late during the day.

At noon, the sun's rays hit the water at a 90-degree angle (more or less, depending on the season and geographic location). Reflection is at a minimum, and depth of penetration is at a maximum. This is why shallow-water fishing is generally poor when the sun is high, unless heavy cloud cover is blocking out the sun's rays.

Using a Depth-o-Lite meter on a very clear lake, I recently made a series of light intensity readings at various depths during selected times of day. The curves shown in the accompanying graph are based on these readings. Notice that there is a sharp drop in all the curves, and that the drop occurs quite deep during most of the day. This sharp drop represents a sort of twilight zone, and this is where the larger bass are more likely to be. At least in theory. When they aren't spawning.

Depth of water. As the graph shows, there are definite relationships between depth of the water, angle of the sun, and light intensity.

These anglers are working the shoreline on the shady side of TVA's Chickamauga Lake. Bass show a marked preference for shade.

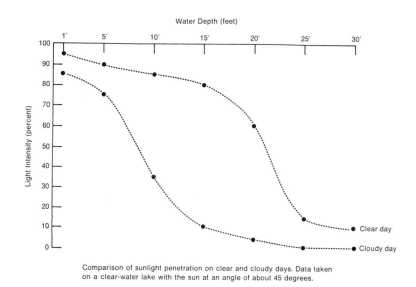

Comparison of sunlight penetration on clear and cloudy days. Data taken on a clear-water lake with the sun at an angle of about 45 degrees.

Since the bass can't regulate the amount of light hitting the retina of the eye, it stands to reason that they will simply go deeper to avoid the bright light. This is generally the case with the larger bass. But there are exceptions. On the clear lake where the readings were taken, I've caught lunker bass at high noon in 5 feet of open water during July, when, according to the theory, they should have been 30 feet down.

Shade and cover. Anything in the water or on the bank that provides shade will of course reduce the underwater light intensity. Shade might be provided by such vegetation as lily pads, by stumps, logs, and timber, or by high bluffs.

The bass angler will do better to fish the shady side of a stream, lake, stump, or dock. Often the shade of a thick tree, such as a cedar, will provide the key to locating bass in other cover or structure. Early or late during the day, the shadow of such a tree will extend far out into the lake or stream, and cover, such as stumps, in this shaded area may be worth concentrating on.

Cloud cover. The position of the sun isn't as important on cloudy, overcast days as it is on bright days, and some of the best bass fishing I've ever had was in shallow water on overcast, misty days. The accompanying graph shows the underwater illumination at 10 A.M. on a sunny day and at 10 A.M. on a cloudy day. These readings were made on a clear lake; they would be lower in murky water.

Wave action. All waves—from gentle ripples to whitecaps—have a bearing on underwater light intensity. During midday, waves tend to impede light ray penetration. Waves cause more refraction and reflection than would occur on a smooth surface. In late afternoon and early morning, however, wave action may cause more underwater illumination than would occur with a smooth surface. When the sun's rays hit at a narrow angle, they tend to reflect. A choppy surface may "catch" some of these rays and direct them downward.

Other aspects of wave action are discussed later in this chapter.

Water clarity. I believe that bass living in a gin-clear lake are more accustomed to high light intensity than bass living in a murky lake, just as a man who works in the out-of-doors is more accustomed to bright daylight than a man who works in a dimly lighted warehouse. For this reason, I don't believe that the ideal light intensity for bass is a fixed value. I suggest that it may well vary from one body of water to another.

In any case, a change in water clarity will often have an effect on bass and their daily habits. Bass will be in shallow water more than usual when a normally clear lake suddenly becomes stained for one reason or another. Top-water lures are often very effective at such times. And the angler should never fail to fish the area where clear water mingles with murky. This interface can sometimes provide fantastic fly-rodding.

Temperature. When I was fishing with one of the bass pros not long ago, I asked him how much importance he placed on water temperature. None whatsoever, he replied. This is a far cry from the advice many of the experts were handing out a few years ago. Shortly after the electronic temperature meters were on the market, a lot of bass anglers—including this one—were spending a lot of time probing the depths for the ideal temperature.

To be sure, I still feel that water temperature is important and has a bearing on how one should fish, but I really don't think it is a reliable indication of where bass will be or won't be. Bass are cold-blooded creatures and probably don't give a damn about temperature, within reasonable limits. In short, I think that dissolved oxygen content, food availability, light intensity, and other variables, together with normal daily and seasonal habits, are far more important than a few degrees of temperature one way or the other. I've caught too many bass in water from 40 to 85 degrees to put much stock in temperature as an indicator of where to find bass.

On the other hand, temperature does affect a bass's metabolic rate and eating habits. Generally, bass in cold water eat less and don't forage about as much, and most knowledgeable bassmen tend to use small, slowly fished lures in cold water. Bass do apparently become sluggish in very warm water, but, as I said, I've caught bass in water up to 85 degrees. (Geographical location might have a lot to do with the upper limit.)

Whenever you do find bass in the ideal temperature range, they'll probably be easier to catch, simply because their metabolism will be at its highest. This temperature range is generally believed to be from 65 to 75 for largemouth bass, 60 to 70 degrees for spots and smallmouth. But I think this ideal range may shift considerably in some lakes. After all, there is a considerable difference in mean temperatures from Mexico to Canada. And if the bass in some of the small, shallow South Florida lakes didn't eat until the temperature dropped into the ideal range, they'd starve to death. I might add that I've caught about a hundred bass from such a lake when the temperature was above the ideal range.

Barometric pressure and weather changes. As compared to the changes in pressure that a bass experiences when it moves only a few feet up or down, changes in barometric pressure are downright infinitesimal. It's my opinion that barometric pressure per se has no influence whatever on bass, on how well they bite or don't bite. On the other hand, cloudy weather associated with rapid changes in barometric pressure can cause bass to feed shallow, and some phenomenal catches of bass have been made when hurricane fronts were moving in.

If I had to draw any conclusions based on my personal experience together with the opinions of others, I would say: Fish deep during high pressure and shallow during low. But take this with a grain or two of salt.

Wind. A warm, sunny afternoon and a calm lake make for good casting conditions, but fishing is often better when there is some wind and wave action. This is especially true in shallow, clear water. Although I am fond of fishing a mirrorlike lake early in the morning and late in the afternoon, I've caught lots of bass—on surface bugs— when the waves were reaching whitecap proportions. It is difficult to fish in such weather, but a bass boat rigged with a bow-mounted electric motor and convenient push-button anchors make it easier, provided that the angler learns to cast a bug in windy weather.

There are several reasons why wave action helps the angler. (1) A ripple on the surface makes it more difficult for bass to see the angler, which can be important in shallow water. (2) Wave action helps oxygenate the water. (3) Waves wash insects and other food across the lake; this attracts bluegills and baitfish, which in turn attract the bass. (4) Wave action gives a surface lure motion and activates hackles and rubber legs on bass bugs. (5) As mentioned earlier in this chapter, ripple on the water can reduce underwater light intensity.

Lunar positions and the solunar theory. I haven't changed my thinking on such matters since I published the following comments in my book *Fishing for Bass:*

Fishing columns in many newspapers, as well as in some of the outdoor magazines, publish daily, weekly, or monthly Solunar Tables. Worked out over three decades ago by John Alden Knight, the tables are based on the changing position of the sun and moon in relation to the earth.

The Solunar Tables show the time of day when feeding activity is likely to be at its peak. Each daily listing includes a major and a minor period for a particular longitude, and the periods for the immediate future can be calculated by adding about fifty minutes per day. If, for example, a minor period is listed for 1:00 P.M. on Monday, the minor will be at 1:50 P.M. on Tuesday and at 2:40 P.M. on Wednesday. A major period lasts from two to three and a half hours; a minor, from three-quarters of an hour to one and a half hours. Although the minor is shorter, bass may sometimes feed more actively than during the major.

Some anglers fish religiously by the major and minor periods, but I personally don't put that much faith in them. I've caught too many lunker bass at times when neither the major nor the minor periods were in effect, and I've too often been skunked during major and minor periods. I do, however, believe that anglers have a better chance of catching bass during a major or minor. But I don't think they should stay off the lake merely because a major or minor isn't in effect. I'm certain that those people who swear by the tables will indeed catch more bass during a major or minor, but I suggest that they probably fish harder and with more confidence during those periods. It is, in my opinion, an error for the bassman to explain success or failure by whether or not the fish are biting. The better philosophy is that the bass will bite at any time of the day or night if the angler can locate them and present the right lure in the right way.

There is no doubt something to the tables, and many anglers can plan their fishing trips accordingly. Believers with enough leisure to choose when they fish should purchase a copy of *Moon Up—Moon Down,* by John Alden Knight. First published in 1942, this 163-page book has recently been reprinted in a limited edition. And the real Solunar enthusiast might want to purchase a Solunagraph wristwatch, available for a mere $195 from Orvis.

Apart from the Solunar tables, some anglers fish by the phases of the moon or by "signs" on calendars and almanacs. Many say, for example, that fishing is best three days before and three days after a full moon. I don't say that these people are loony, but again I don't believe a man ought to stay at home because the moon is full or isn't full.

Water flow. Most anglers don't realize it, but water flow can be extremely important when they are fishing on some impoundments. If the turbines and gates are shut off, there may be little or no flow. But if the turbines are operating or the gates are open, or both, water will flow to some degree throughout the impoundment; and there will be more flow in the river and creek channels. In coastal regions, brackish-water bass tend to hit best on a rising tide, and the water flow no doubt has something to do with this. I don't know exactly why flow should be so important, but I submit the following thoughts on the matter:

1. A flow washes bits of food about, which in turn makes crayfish, minnows, and so forth more active.

2. The bass in most impoundments are from the original stream or river, so that a flow is a natural condition for them; static water, unnatural.

3. A flow may help oxygenate the water, or, rather, cause more water (and therefore more oxygen) to pass over the bass's gills. I talked with one expert smallmouth angler who seemed to think that bass can be sort of hyped up during major flow periods.

For whatever reason, bass will sometimes quit biting when the flow is stopped. I mean totally quit. If you can pick your time to fish a certain impoundment, it might be a good idea to see whether draw-down schedules are available. I hate to suggest it, but it wouldn't surprise me to see any day now an ad in *BASSmaster Magazine* for an electronic flow probe. We've got everything else.

11

Fishing Shorelines and Visible Cover

AT ONE TIME, just about all bass fishing was done along the shoreline. Then deepwater-structure fishing came into vogue, and a lot of bassmen, armed with depth finders and temperature probes and other new gadgets, started looking for hot spots all over the lake. They found them. A lot of pluggers of the old school felt left out; not having anything to cast toward, they simply didn't like to fish in open water and were reluctant about plugging the shoreline and grass beds because they felt that they were missing the real action. The fact is, however, that the expert bass angler can do very well indeed by casting to visible cover. John Powell and other bassmen have proved this, time after time, by winning major bass tournaments by fishing in shallow water.

I feel that the fly-rodder, too, will do well to specialize in shallow water, and that he can often outfish hardware slingers. Here are some likely spots to try:

Stumps. Any stump along a shoreline is enough to perk a bass angler's interest. Individual stumps aren't likely to hold a group of bass at any one time, but a good stump can pay off over the years.

A nice bass from a Florida lake. Note the stumps in the background.

As soon as a bass is caught from around a good stump, another one is likely to move in. Of course, one stump might not be as good as another, and remember that visible stumps in a heavily fished lake, impoundment, or stream are fished by every angler that comes along. Some of the most productive stumps are those that are normally submerged, and marking these carefully during low-water periods will surely pay off during subsequent fishing trips.

Stump fields in impoundments, made by cutting timber before the land was flooded, are another matter. For one reason or another, individual stumps in such fields may be better than others, and, also, one stump field, or section of a field, may not be as good as another.

Stump field

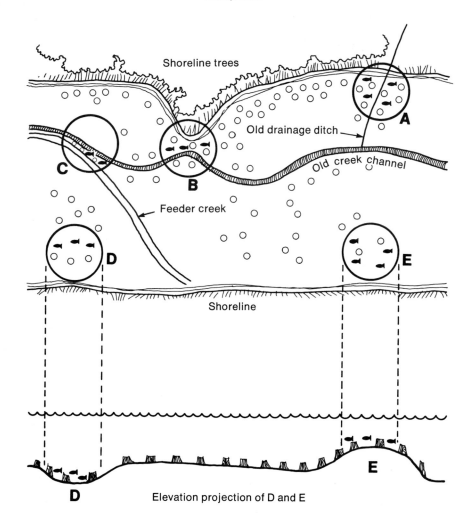

Shoreline trees

Old drainage ditch

Old creek channel

Feeder creek

C

B

A

D

E

Shoreline

D   Elevation projection of D and E   E

Take a look at the accompanying diagram. Assume that the stumps are in shallow water, and then consider related structure. While it's true that all the stumps might hold bass, the angler would increase his chances by concentrating on points A, B, C, D, and E.

The drainage ditch or draw from the river channel to A could serve as an excellent migration route; this, in turn, could mean that the stumps around A might provide excellent fishing when the bass are feeding. The point at B might also be a good spot, especially since the point is near a bend in the creek. Stumps at C, which might well be submerged, could be very good; the point where two stream beds meet is always worth investigating.

Depth variations can also cause bass to gather at a certain cluster of stumps, as shown at D and E. Generally, the fly-rodder will be more interested in E—and often the bass will be, too.

Logs and treetops. Individual logs and trees, as distinguished from submerged stands of timber, that have fallen into the water along the bank often provide excellent bass hangouts, especially in natural lakes and streams. They are sometimes good in impoundments, but flooded timber in many impoundments rather distracts from the importance of a single tree or log.

When fishing a log, remember that the bass will usually be either under it or lying on the shady side of it. Choose your casts accordingly, and try to avoid hooking the bass on the far side of the log. Retrieving a lure parallel to the log may pay off, but remember that the bass will usually be looking out toward open water instead of facing the bank. Therefore, if you are fishing from a boat and cast parallel to the log and toward the bank, you'll throw the bug behind the fish, and might well spook it. Usually, it's best to cast short of the mark, fish the lure a few feet, then pick up and cast a little farther. And so on until you have fished the length of the log. If the log submerges, try to project it mentally and fish it out accordingly.

Fallen treetops are often better than logs, but they are more difficult to fish thoroughly. As was pointed out in Chapter 8, it is best to cast toward the base of the tree, or toward the base of any particular limb, in order to avoid hanging the lure. Also consider what can happen when you hook a lunker bass in a treetop. If you cast perpendicular to the trunk of the tree, a hooked bass can easily get under something. If you cast toward the top of the tree, the bass can dive and catch the line in a fork. But if you cast toward the base of the trunk, or limb, you'll have a much better chance of working the bass out. Also, it is best to make your first casts around the outer perimeter of the limbs, then work on back toward the trunk.

Grass beds and lily pads. Weeds, grass beds, and lily pads provide cover and shade for bass when they are in shallow water. Often such vegetation is the only sort of cover available in natural lakes.

One way to fish such cover is to move rather fast until you locate the fish. Then slow down. It is usually best, however, to concentrate on cover near deep water or near a migration route, if available.

After you have selected a likely patch of pads or a grass bed, pay attention to irregularities such as pockets, potholes, and points. Quite often a productive spot is where two kinds of cover meet. I've had good luck where grass meets lily pads, and where boat lanes have been cut through such cover.

Often, a weed bed along a shoreline will have an outside and an inside edge. As a general rule, larger bass will be near the outside. But there are enough exceptions to disprove this rule, especially very early and very late during the day, at night, and during the spawning season.

I always thoroughly fish a small patch of vegetation set apart from

A fly-rodder and his guide work the shoreline of Currituck Sound, a great spot for brackish-water largemouth.

the main bunch, except when the sun is high, and this has paid off for me nicely. Over a period of 4 years, I caught at least a dozen bass from 7 pounds on up to 11 from a little clump of lily pads no larger than a coffee table. I've also had good fishing around a small patch of grass isolated from the main bed.

I recently read that lily pads are very poor cover, and that bass won't hang out in pads if any other cover is available. This hasn't been my experience. I've seen some patches of pads that were very, very good at certain times of the year. But I've also seen acres of pads that weren't worth a damn.

Still another type of cover that is sometimes available is grass or moss that grows on the bottom but doesn't reach the surface. Poppers and streamers will sometimes produce when fished over such cover, but I prefer to use a spinner attachment, not so much because of the flash but because I believe the sonic vibration may rouse a bass from out of holes in the vegetation.

Lures and tactics for fishing in vegetation were discussed in Chapter 8.

Brush and stickups. Any sort of brush in shallow water may hold bass, but the angler will do well to concentrate on bushes and larger areas of brush near deep water, a migration route, or some such feature, as discussed previously under Stumps.

When fishing this type of cover, it's best to get the lure into it; consequently, a keel fly or weedless bug will usually be in order, depending on how thick the cover is. Also try small weedlessly rigged plastic worms and pork strips.

When fishing a shoreline, keep an eye peeled for stickups out in the lake. Such a stickup will often indicate slightly submerged cover. If you don't know whether a stickup indicates a single bush or a patch of brush, it will pay you to find out. Use a sinking weedless lure to feel out the area on all sides of the stick-up. Many bassmen are expert at using plastic worms to "read" cover and lake bottoms.

Pockets and draws. Any pocket in the shoreline, or in such cover as grass beds, is worth casting into. How good a pocket is often depends on the depth of the water, and how many casts you make into a pocket depends largely on its size. Some draws will require a number of casts to fish them out thoroughly.

In small pockets, say 1 foot wide and 3 feet deep, I usually make at least two casts. The first is made to the mouth; the second, to the back of the pocket. Presenting the lure delicately and fishing it gently is often the key to catching bass in small pockets. A noisy approach may frighten the bass out of the pocket, especially if the water is shallow and clear. I might add that small pockets have been very productive for me, especially for largemouth.

Coves. In large impoundments, and in some natural lakes, more fishing is done in coves than in other places of comparable surface area. The reason isn't necessarily because more fish are in coves, but because the wind and water are normally calmer. This can be a big advantage to the fly caster, especially if he doesn't have a large, fully rigged bass boat; but calm water doesn't necessarily make for the best bass fishing.

It is, of course, usually advisable to pick coves carefully, looking for cover, structure, and substructure as discussed throughout this chapter and the next. I prefer coves with old creek channels running through them, or with vegetation or some such cover along the banks. Either new water from a creek or ample vegetation can raise the oxygen content of cove water to a level higher than that out in the main body of the lake or impoundment. Also, the temperature in a cove can vary considerably from that in the main lake; generally, a cove tends to warm up faster in spring and cool off faster in fall, which can mean that cove fishing is better during spring and fall, at least in some areas. But don't overlook the back end of coves on warm, sunny days during the dead of winter.

Run-ins. Don't ever neglect to cast to the mouth of a branch or drainage ditch. Bass often lie around such spots, especially after or during a rain, watching for food washing down. Often a change in water clarity, temperature, or oxygen content will attract and hold bass around a run-in. In brackish water, a change in salinity can attract bass.

The mouth of canals and overflow ditches should also be fished, although they may be "run-outs." Causeway bridges or culverts in lakes and impoundments will often have water flowing one way or the other, depending on wind and wave action. Fishing them accordingly will sometimes pay off. There is a little bridge on the causeway out to my island house, and the leeward side is almost always good for at least one bass.

Bluffs and ledges. Any bluff or ledge is likely to hold bass—especially spots. They are, however, difficult to fish with a fly rod. If the bass are near the surface, then such a bank can be fished normally. But remember that the water is likely to be quite deep, and that the bass may be in underlying pockets, so that surface lures may not do the trick.

If surface lures fail to produce, the best bet (with a fly rod) is to hold the boat close to the bluff and fish parallel to it. Try a worm, weighted streamer, or some such sinking lure; cast ahead of the boat and tight-line the lure down instead of retrieving it. On the next cast, place your lure 5 feet or so ahead of the first cast, and again tight-line the lure down. And so on from one end of the bluff to the other.

Rocks. Any sort of rocky structure or bottom may attract bass, especially in lakes and impoundments where soft mud bottoms predominate. Large single boulders, as well as rock piles, along the shore or in shallow water should always be fished. Lake bottoms composed of gravel or cert may hold bass, especially if most of the lake bottom is mud; but it's better to have some sort of additional cover or structure.

The riprap on dams or along causeways can be very productive at times.

Bottom changes. Be alert for *any* changes in the composition of a lake bottom, as, for example, where a mud bottom gives way to sand. It's best to have some sort of cover at the juncture, but this isn't absolutely necessary. I've caught bass in "clean" bare areas at lakeside homes.

Often the bank can provide tips on such bottom changes, so be observant. Also, a good flasher-type depth finder can alert the angler to the nature of the bottom, if he knows how to read the signals.

Submerged man-made structure. Usually, such structure as houses and barns that have been inundated are associated with deep, open water. The bassman should, however, take advantage of any such structure along the shoreline. For example, where old roadbeds enter the water might be good spots for bass, especially if old ditches are present on either side. Fencerows can also be good.

Docks, piers, boathouses, etc. Almost any sort of dock or other structure that extends out over the water provides good shade and cover for bass. If given a choice, I prefer to fish a dock at a vacation home rather than at a permanent residence. My thinking is that constant use tends to scare really big bass away. On the other hand, many people feed bread and table scraps to the fish. This draws bluegills, shiners, minnows, and such, which in turn draw bass.

Another reason for fishing around piers and docks is that people often sink down brush, old tires, and such stuff nearby. These "artificial reefs" are usually intended to draw crappie, but they are also excellent bass attractors as well.

Although I do fish piers and other such structures near a residence, I don't feel quite right about it. I've had too many people fishing in my lakeside backyard, and more than once worm fishermen have banged hunks of lead against my boat. I don't really object to a bass-man fishing out my backyard and moving on, but it does rub me the wrong way for a guy to anchor 10 yards off my patio when I'm out drinking my morning coffee. I don't own the lake, though, and don't have the gall of one of my neighbors, who comes out the door in polka-dot pajamas saying, "Good morning, sports fans!"

Dams. Any dam, from farm ponds on up to huge impoundments, can provide excellent bass fishing, and I am especially fond of those with riprap. Note the slope of the dam and fish accordingly. Pay particular attention to the spot where the dam joins the bank. If you are out in a boat and casting to a dam, try a soggy muddler minnow. Pop it a couple of times on the surface, then let it sink down. A slow, steady retrieve will usually keep the muddler bumping along the riprap.

Points. Some bass anglers more or less specialize in fishing points, and some of the tournament pros have made a career of it. The fly-rodder could do far worse, but fishing points thoroughly with a fly rod is more difficult than it is with spinning and baitcasting rigs, simply because the points that are visible from along the bank often extend far out into the lake or impoundment. Still, some very good surface and shallow fishing can be found along points. But one point may not be as good as another.

Consider the accompanying diagram. Point A might be good because, as shown by the contour lines, it extends out near the creek channel. Point B would likely be relatively unproductive. Point C could be a good spot for bass, but it would be easier to fish it properly with spinning or baitcasting gear by bumping a jig or other heavy lure down it—or up it.

Point D would be likely to hold bass because it is so close to the creek channel. Point E might be good because the lily pads and grass provide cover. The grass on the point extension should be fished thoroughly. Typically, I'll fish around the edge of grass points, then move in and fish the middle of it if I can get a keel streamer or weedless lure down in the water.

Point F wouldn't likely be a good spot, but point G, also in shallow water, might be good because of the hard, rocky bottom.

Points

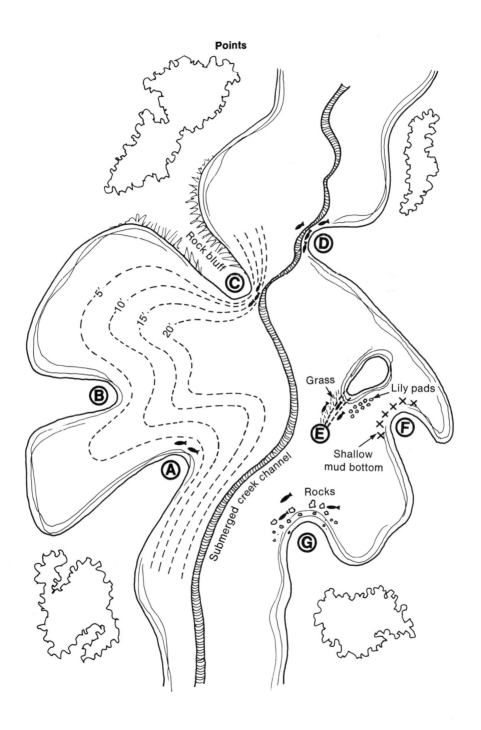

In addition to land points, also keep an eye out for points in grass beds, weeds, stump fields, and so on.

Also, remember that bass tend to congregate at points, so that if you catch one there may be others. This is especially true of points near deep water, as at C and D. (If bass are at A or F, they'll likely be scattered and feeding instead of holding.) If you do find a congregation of bass, don't spook them. Some bass experts have caught 70 or 80 pounds of lunker bass from a single hot spot!

12

Fishing Open Water

ANYONE WHO TAKES A FLY ROD into midlake and starts casting randomly is pretty much wasting good fishing time. He might luck into a school of bass, or some suspended bass, and he might even hit a veritable hot spot on the bottom. But it would be blind luck, and expert bassmen proceed on more scientific footing.

Whichever way you choose to fish in open water—casting, trolling, or yo-yoing—locating structure and substructure is the key to success. A good depth finder is almost indispensable, and a good topographic or contour map will save you some time. Look especially for:

Creek channels. Although creek channels are often difficult to fish thoroughly with a fly rod, they are probably the favorite type of structure among bassmen. For one thing, they are relatively easy to find and follow because they will be well marked on topographic maps.

There are several reasons why submerged creek channels are such good bass habitat. (1) The creek was running through the area

Large impoundments built all over the country have greatly increased bass habitat, especially for the largemouth. Kentucky Dam, shown here, backs up water for 184 miles, thereby creating excellent submerged structure as well as a thousand miles of shoreline.

many years before the impoundment was made, and will usually have eroded the land or rock so that the channel makes for drastic changes in depth. (2) Creek channels usually provide both cover and shade. (3) The channel is an excellent migration route from the main lake into the backside of associated coves. (4) Because the creek channel existed before the impoundment was made, it is a natural spot for bass. (5) The creek bed usually makes a break in the surrounding structure; if it ran through woods, for example, its sandbars, rock shoals, and so on will be different from the flooded timber or remaining stumps. (6) The creek and river channels will be spots of maximum water flow in the impoundment.

If you want to fish a creek bed with your fly rod, remember that some parts of it may be better than others. It's best to concentrate on the outside bends and on the areas indicated on the accompanying diagram.

Deep holes. Very often deep holes will attract bass, especially in natural lakes without much structure. Usually, a saucer-shaped hole without any substructure isn't ideal; a hole with a sharp drop on one or more sides will be a better prospect. Anyhow, the area around the edge of the deep hole should be fished thoroughly; most of the large bass I've caught in natural lakes have been near, but not in, deep holes.

Submerged islands. Any rise, knoll, or sunken island in a lake or impoundment may provide excellent bass fishing. I would, in fact, rather fish an island than a pothole. Knolls and islands are often especially productive if they occur in other structure, such as flooded timber or stump fields or creek channels. Sometimes you can find a knoll in a deep hole, and this situation can be hot indeed.

Often an island will come to within a few feet of the surface, and such spots may prove to be prime bedding areas during spawning season. Some islands may have grass growing above the surface, and these are usually ideal for fly-rodding.

Points and draws. Any flooded point or draw can be a potential hot spot. Often, points that are visible on land will extend far out into a lake or impoundment.

Springs. Underwater springs may be extremely good for bass, but they are difficult to locate. Sometimes, however, they will be indicated on topographic maps.

Rock bottom. Rocky bottoms will hold bass, especially in a natural lake that is pretty much covered with mud and moss. In fact, any change in the bottom may attract bass, even far out in the lake.

Ledges. Underwater ledges will sometimes be very good for bass, especially spots. But they are usually difficult to fish with a fly rod. Yo-yoing might work.

Timber. Sometimes timber is left standing in an impoundment and it often provides good bass fishing. If the bass are deep in heavy timber, about the only way to get a lure to them is by yo-yoing. Often, however, bass will be suspended in timber, so that surface bugs and streamers may produce. Sputterbuzzing a spinner along the surface may be very effective at times for suspended bass. A good deal depends on how deep they are.

In large areas of timber, it's best to look for substructure or try to find a pattern. Such substructure might be a rise in the timber (caused by a knoll on the bottom), which can sometimes be detected without a depth finder simply by looking at the height of the trees. A pattern might be established if, for example, you catch a bass from a certain kind of treetop or at a certain depth. Effective patterns may vary from day to day, or from one time of day to another.

Man-made structure. Submerged buildings, fencerows, roadbeds, bridges, culverts, dams from old farm ponds, etc., are excellent structure for bass. Bridges and culverts can be very good, but they are difficult to fish with a fly. Roadbeds are sometimes productive, and are easy to locate with the aid of depth finders and topographic maps, or merely by noting where an old road enters or leaves an impoundment. When fishing roads, however, it is best to look for substructure or unusual features, such as sharp bends, S-curves, high road banks, hills, and so on.

Stickups. Any twig or limb sticking out of the water may indicate potentially good bass fishing. Stickups from submerged brush, willow trees, and so on should be of especial interest to fly-rodders because they will be in rather shallow water. Stickups in flats may be exceptionally good during the spawning season, and sometimes acre after acre of such flats are productive.

I'll usually start with poppers and other surface lures around stickups. If they don't produce, I'll tie on a keel fly and spinner, fishing 3 or 4 feet deep. As a last resort, I'll go to weedlessly rigged worms or pork eels.

When you are fishing large areas of stickups, it's best to move along pretty fast until you locate the bass. One effective lure is the tiny jig, light trailer, and doglegged spinner arm. It can be buzzed along the

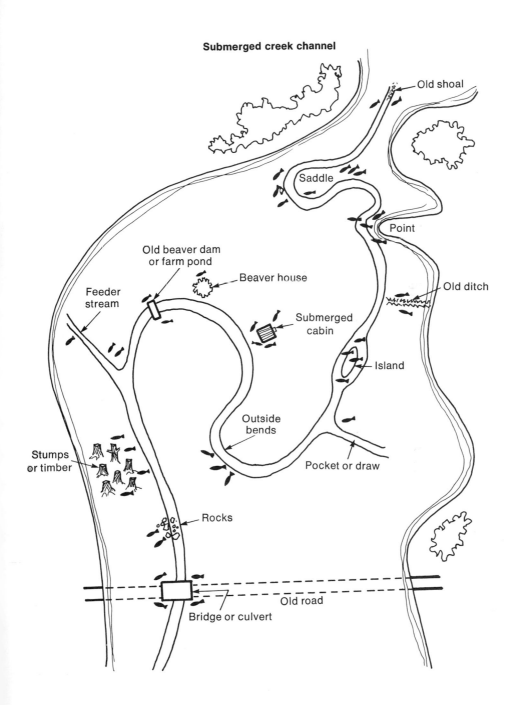

Submerged creek channel

Old shoal

Saddle

Point

Old beaver dam
or farm pond

Beaver house

Old ditch

Feeder
stream

Submerged
cabin

Island

Outside
bends

Pocket or draw

Stumps
or timber

Rocks

Old road

Bridge or culvert

surface or fished on down to any depth. Although the rig is difficult to cast, it is excellent for covering a large area fast, from top to bottom.

There is one type of offshore fishing that can be done without a depth finder, topographic maps, and other such aids. But you will need a fast boat. I'm talking about jump fishing for schooling bass. The idea is to ride around on the boat until you spot schooling activity, then run in close enough to cast, cut the motor, and start fishing as quickly as possible—before the school sounds.

Actually, the bass aren't really schooling; they're feeding on bait-fish, usually shad. Consequently, jump fishing is usually better on lakes or impoundments with large shad populations. Schooling can also occur in rivers, although the action isn't usually good enough to justify jump fishing. Moreover, really good jump fishing is pretty much a southern sport, although bass do school to some extent in large lakes and impoundments north of the Mason-Dixon line.

Jump fishing can be good in spring, summer, and fall, depending on the particular impoundment or lake, and it is often better during the middle of the day. Consequently, if you plan to be on a lake all day and have a fast bass boat, you might bug the shoreline during early morning, chase the schools during the middle of the day, and return to the shore line in late afternoon.

As I pointed out in Chapter 6, it is often important that the angler match whatever the schooling bass are feeding on, not only in profile but also in length. Streamers, bucktails, and ultralight spoons are in my opinion better than plugs, and this makes the fly rod a good choice for jump fishing. It's a different sort of casting, however, from working a shoreline or casting to any sort of cover. The angler should learn to shoot line out quickly, with a minimum of false casts, before the school sounds. It's best to keep the fly line neatly coiled on the boat deck, so that you'll be ready when the action starts. Distance casting helps, but accuracy isn't usually too important. Any fly-rodder who wants to try jump fishing should consider investing in a shooting head and a rod fitted with aluminum oxide rings. He might also consider a bass boat with a removable seat on the fishing deck. And then he might take a tip from Charles Waterman and put a plastic garbage can up there to hold his shooting line, if nobody is looking.

Polarized sunglasses will help you spot schooling activity, and binoculars will greatly extend your range. Also, be on the lookout for swooping gulls and other birds that feed on baitfish.

See Chapter 6 for a discussion of lures, retrieves, and other matters relating to catching schooling bass. I might add here that schooling bass will sometimes hit any reasonable offering, but if they don't hit whatever you are throwing them within three or four casts, try something else. I've seen guys, even fly-rodders, cast for an hour into a school of bass without a strike. It can be frustrating, to say the least.

Part Four

The Mechanics
of
Fly Fishing

WHEN I FIRST STARTED outlining this book, I planned to put some simple beginner's casting instructions in an appendix and let it go at that. My thinking was that people who already know how to cast would thereby be spared the details in the main body of the book. After watching dozens of bass anglers at work, however, I decided that the instructions should definitely be a real part of the text itself instead of being stuck back in an appendix.

In addition to instructing rank beginners, I hope that the following chapters will help make casting easier to those who have been thrashing about for years. Casting a fly for normal distances should be an almost effortless process. If an angler tires quickly from fly casting, either he doesn't have balanced tackle or he needs to work on his style.

13

Casting a Line

THE BEST WAY TO LEARN to cast is to attend a good school, such as those conducted by Orvis and Fenwick, or to get some personal guidance from an expert. But this isn't necessary. Whatever skill I have with a fly rod has been acquired without personal instruction. I simply bought an outfit, carefully read what the manufacturer's booklets said, and started casting. I might add that I was catching fish (bluegill, mostly) on my rig within two hours after I put a line onto the reel. To be sure, I wasn't getting distance or shooting line, and my style left a lot to be desired. But the fact remains that I was casting a bug out and catching fish. Shortly thereafter, fortunately, I did receive some good advice from a competent fly caster who watched me in action.

I think I picked up elementary fly casting easily because (1) I had formed reasonably good habits with spinning and baitcasting rigs, (2) I believed the fly-casting instructions, and (3) I tried to analyze what went wrong on an unsuccessful cast so that I could do better next time. If my experience at teaching others to cast is any indication, some anglers have trouble with a fly rod because (1) they ac-

146

quired bad habits from baitcasting and spinning in which they incorrectly sling lures out instead of truly casting them, (2) they don't understand the principles of fly casting and therefore don't fully believe the instructions, and (3) after an unsuccessful cast they merely try harder to force the bug out instead of stopping to think about what they are doing, or not doing.

Not long ago, I tried to teach a stubborn fellow how to cast a bug. After he had watched me make a couple of casts, he said it didn't look as though there were much to it. (There's not.) He took the rod, snatched the bug out of the water, slung the rod behind him, and swished it forward. Line, leader, and bug collapsed in a heap onto the water short of the mark. I told him that he hadn't stopped the rod overhead and hadn't waited for the line to straighten out on the backcast. He stood up, snatched the line out of the water, slung the rod over his shoulder, and put all the muscle he had into the forward cast, determined to sling that damned bug out. Since he got the backcast off to a bad start, this cast was even more disastrous. Line and leader and bug fell all over the boat. I repeated my instructions, but he didn't pay any attention and kept flogging away. I said no more until the guy convinced himself that he couldn't get the bug out. Once he accepted the fact that he needed help, we started over and he was casting fairly well within a few minutes.

Most of the casting instructions I've seen advise the beginner to practice on a smooth, freshly cut lawn or some such surface with 80 feet or so of clearance. This is probably sound advice, but I learned on the water simply because I lived beside a lake and had trees all over my yard. I don't think it makes too much difference where one starts, but I do think that the beginner should be standing instead of sitting on a boat seat. I also advise the beginner to start with a small fly instead of a large bug—and that he snip off the business end of the hook.

Although the motion involved in fly casting should not be jerky, it can, for the sake of discussion, be broken down into steps and phases. Before discussing these more fully, however, I would like to refer to the clock-dial illustrations on the next page and run through a simple cast.

Facing the 9 o'clock position, the angler works out about 30 feet of fly line. (For his first practice cast, he can simply strip the line off the reel and walk it out directly in front of him.) Pointing the rod pretty much toward the lure, he starts the pickup by raising the rod tip

The back cast

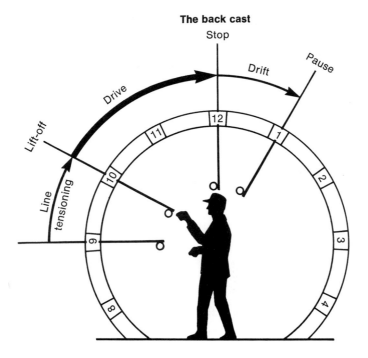

The forward cast

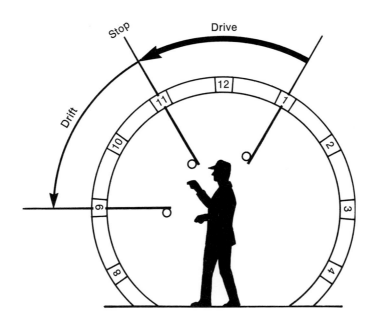

progressively. When the tip is at about 10 o'clock, he accelerates the rod, picking the line up and casting it overhead. This power stroke continues to the 12 o'clock position. Then the rod is stopped. Stopped dead. Directly over his head. The fly line is still in motion, however, and the caster must pause until the line straightens out behind him. This pause is absolutely necessary. After the stop, however, and during the pause, the angler lets the rod drift back to about 1 o'clock. (Distance casters may drift back farther, but beginners should stop at 1 o'clock.) When the angler feels the line load the rod, he proceeds with the forward cast, driving the rod to 11 o'clock. The fly line goes forward, carrying the leader and lure with it. Note that the line must turn over on the forward cast (and on the backcast); consequently, the line will form a loop during its course.

The backcast is the key to fly-fishing, and a good backcast almost assures a passable forward cast. But remember that the backcast is not complete unless the line straightens out behind the angler. If the pause is too long, however, the line and leader will touch down. Although a number of fish and possibly a water skier or two have been caught by default on the backcast, the angler will do well to keep the line above the water and out of the bushes.

Anyhow, the simple instructions given above are all an angler needs to start casting a fly, provided that his gear is matched pretty well. If the angler should cast very long on such simple instruction, however, he might form a few bad habits that he would later regret. I would therefore like to go into more detail on some of the various phases and steps of the cast, together with some related topics.

The grip. Hold the rod firmly, but not tensely in the right hand (left if you are left-handed). Most fly-rodders place the thumb on top of the handle, as shown in the photograph on page 150. But a few anglers prefer to have the thumb at the side, and some who use short rods and light lines find that they can present a dry fly more delicately with the index finger on top of the handle. Any grip that is comfortable throughout the cast is all right, but I do recommend the one shown in the photograph.

The pivot points. Using the wrist as a pivot point is extremely tiring if the angler makes repeated casts with gear heavy enough to handle large bass bugs. Although some trout anglers who work small streams may still use the wrist, most modern casters keep the wrist stiff (except when the rod is drifting). Thus, the rod becomes an extension of the forearm.

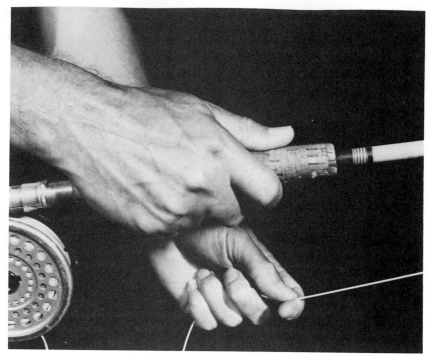

The usual grip for casting.

If the angler keeps his wrist stiff, the elbow then becomes the pivot point. This permits the use of the arm muscles, which are both long and strong as compared to the short muscles brought into play by a flick of the wrist.

I recommend that the beginner keep his elbow at his side during the cast, but this isn't a hard and fast rule. Many experts raise the elbow during the cast, especially if they are going for distance. I feel, however, that the angler who gets his regular casting down pat will unconsciously modify or adjust the elbow movement, as required. Note that even if the expert caster raises his elbow, it is still the pivot point for the forearm and rod. When he raises his elbow, then, he is simply changing the position of the pivot point. Anyhow, I recommend that the beginner practice with his elbow at his side until he gets his timing down pat.

Making the backcast. Too many bass anglers snatch their bugs out of the water instead of picking them up smoothly. The trick is to start the lure moving until the rod is at about 10 o'clock, then lift it

off with a smooth, accelerating power stroke. Continue this movement—an upward lift, forceful, with a stiff wrist—until the rod is
directly overhead. Then stop the rod. Some anglers, probably the ma-
jority, actually stop the rod at the 1 o'clock position or even later, but
the beginner will do well to concentrate on 12 o'clock, sharp. (He is
likely to wind up at 1 or 2 o'clock anyway.) In time this stop will come
naturally, and I suspect that the ideal stopping point will vary slightly
not only from angler to angler but also with various rods and lines.
When I'm casting with my 1¾-ounce graphite rod, I actually stop at a
few minutes before 12; with my 6¼-ounce fiberglass rod, I normally
stop at a little after 12.

Most anglers let the rod drift back to 1 o'clock, or even 2 o'clock, but
this movement is only a drift, does not exert any force on the line, and
occurs only after a definite stop, although it may appear to be a continuous power stroke to an untrained eye.

Note: All the motions and application of power from the pickup
until the stop should *not* be directed toward casting the line behind
you. Instead, try to cast the line high into the air. This will help with
making the stop and will help keep the backcast up where it ought
to be.

The pause and drift. After you have stopped the rod directly
overhead, you *must* pause while the line straightens out behind you.
If you begin the forward cast too early, your backcast will be aborted
and your rod won't be loaded properly. In effect, this is similar to
putting a spinning or baitcasting plug on the ground with several
feet of slack line, and then trying to cast it out. If the plug doesn't
load the rod, you can't cast it effectively; if the fly line doesn't load
the rod, you can't cast it effectively either, no matter how hard you
try.

The length of the pause will vary with the amount of line out, the
weight and wind resistance of the lure, and other factors. It is therefore not a stopwatch matter. When the line straightens out, however,
it will exert a discernible tug on the rod. The experienced angler
senses this and automatically begins the forward cast when he feels it.
Beginners often have difficulty here; they don't quite get the message
and pause too long or, as more often happens, they don't wait long
enough. The best bet is to look over your shoulder and watch the line
straighten out. Soon you'll gain confidence and will believe the slight
tug when you feel it.

After you get the stop and the pause down pat, you'll probably start opening your wrist slightly to permit the rod to drift back. You might also raise your elbow up, in a sort of arm-cocking motion in anticipation of the forward cast, especially if you have to make a long or difficult cast into the wind. I think that both of these motions are natural and shouldn't be of too much concern to the beginner. At first, concentrate on the 12 o'clock stop and the pause.

The forward cast. It has been said that if you make a good back-cast, a decent forward cast will be almost automatic. There's a lot of truth in the statement, but the forward cast shouldn't be taken for granted.

A common mistake is to bring the rod down instead of forward. A downward stroke applies the power while the rod is going through a wide arc, which in turn results in a wide loop. A wide loop is indicative of a slow, inaccurate cast that is not good for getting distance or going into the wind.

Anyhow, the better way is to drive the rod forward, and keep the

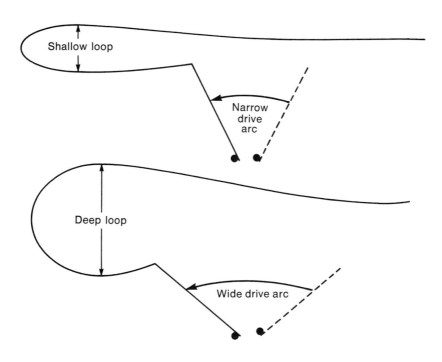

arc narrow. Stop the rod at about 11 o'clock, then open the wrist, and let the rod drift down to about 9:30 while the line is straightening out.

The hammer analogy is often used to illustrate the forward power stroke, and I would like to repeat it here, briefly. Start driving a nail into a wall at eye level. Stand a foot and a half back from the wall. To drive such a nail from this position, you would first draw the hammer back over your shoulder to about 1 o'clock and then drive it forward until it hit the nail and stopped at about 11 o'clock. Try it, and remember the analogy when you practice your forward stroke. (Actually, the hammer analogy also applies to the backcast, except that you would be hitting a nail slightly behind your head.)

The forward stop is important for casting a fast line, although the principle is a little difficult to understand fully. For one thing, stopping the rod at 11 o'clock keeps the arc narrow and the loop tight—but there's more to it than that. I think it is safe to say that the stop forces the rod to "unload," which in turn accelerates the fly line.

Releasing line. Throughout the cast, the left hand should keep the line under tension and should pretty much follow the movements of the rod hand. If you want to shoot line for a longer cast, the time to do so is at the completion of the forward power stroke. The line to be released, of course, must be stripped off the reel and should be loose at your feet, held loosely in your line hand, or coiled in a stripping basket. Most bass anglers keep a goodly length of working line off their reel, and they adjust the length of their casts by stripping in line before the backcast or by shooting line out with the forward cast.

If you want to release more line than you can shoot out on the cast, you can do so by false-casting. To make a false cast, proceed with the backcast and forward cast as normal, but pick the line up for another cast before the lure or line touches down. The idea, of course, is to release line on each false cast until you can get the bug out as far as you want it. False casts can also be used to dry out flies and deer-hair bugs.

Presenting the lure. After the angler gets the basics of casting down pat, he'll slowly discover that the fly rod is more accurate than even a baitcasting rig. He might also discover that he can present the lure more gently than he can with either baitcasting or spinning gear, and the comparatively light weight of the bass bug or fly isn't the only reason.

I feel that accuracy will come in time, but gentle presentation may not. The trick is to aim the bug a foot or so above the target. If you aim right at the target, say a small pocket in lily pads, the bug will shoot in and splat down. If you aim high and the cast goes well, your line will go out with the leader and bug following. Toward the end of the cast, the fly line will straighten out, transmitting the energy to the leader. The leader and bug will turn over and all the energy will be expended in midair, just over the pocket. The bug will simply alight on the water. It's beautiful. Pure poetry, etc. More important, such a presentation is likely to attract a bass instead of spooking it, especially in shallow water.

Fancy pickups. I'm fond of fishing my bug or lure on the pickup, and therefore I usually avoid anything fancy. There are times, however, when a normal pickup will get you in trouble or just won't do the job. If, for example, you cast over a partly submerged log, a normal pickup may well hang up your bug. The same problem may occur if your fly line gets under a lily pad, or if you cast into rather thick grass. Here are a few tricks to try when the need arises:

The snake pickup. Start this move by holding the rod out in front of you and parallel to the water. Wave the tip from side to side just before and during the pickup. This sends S-curves down the line, and these curves will lift leader and lure out of the water on the pickup.

The half-roll pickup. Start a roll cast as described in Chapter 15. While the lure and leader are in the air toward the end of the roll, make a regular pickup for the backcast. (When making the roll, do not let the rod drift down past 10:30 after the power stroke has been applied.) The half-roll pickup is excellent for getting a sinking line out of the water in preparation for a regular pickup.

The snap pickup. Hold the rod at 10 o'clock and raise it to 11. Then snap it back to 10. This movement will send a hump down the line, which in turn will lift the lure off the water. At that point, you pick up as usual for the backcast. The snap pickup is very good for getting flies and bugs over obstructions.

I would like to point out that many bass anglers make too many casts that are too short. Casts of, say, only 20 feet will tire the angler quicker than normal casts of 40 feet. The reason is that the angler doesn't have enough fly line out to load the rod properly. Fly rods are designed to carry the first 30 or 35 feet of a fly line, and if less line is out the rod is simply underloaded. This is almost like trying to cast a ¼-ounce lure with a baitcasting rod designed for ½-ounce lures.

Short casts are, of course, sometimes necessary, as when fishing some small streams. But many bassmen, when they begin to tire from repeated casts, tend to inch their boats in closer to the bank or cover when they might actually cast with less effort if they would get farther out. They'll catch more bass, too, if they make casts of normal length—especially if they are standing or fishing from a bass boat with high deck-mounted pedestal seats.

14

Getting Distance and Beating the Wind

THE MOST ENJOYABLE WAY to fish a bug with a fly rod is to make casts of about 40 feet, and normally this is enough distance between the angler and the lure. It is not too difficult to cast even a large bug farther than 40 feet, but it does become tiring to pick up and cast a lot of fly line for fast, repeated cycles. The bass angler usually fishes a bug only a few feet before the pickup, which means that he wants to make lots of casts per hour. Subsurface lures, of course, can be fished on in, but retrieving a surface bug more than 3 or 4 feet is pretty much a waste of time in most cases. Even if you do retrieve a bass bug in close, you'll have to false-cast to get it out again. So working the boat along about 40 feet out from the shoreline or cover saves the bassman a lot of time and effort.

But it is good to know how to make longer casts should the need arise. Casting 70 or 80 feet, or even 100, is not unreasonable if you have the proper gear and aren't trying to throw the largest bug in your tackle box. The secret is in increasing line speed, keeping a tight loop, and learning to handle shooting line smoothly. It is also very important that you have adequate and balanced gear, as discussed in Part One.

156

There are several tricks that experienced casters use to increase line speed without overly exerting themselves. But I would like to emphasize at this point that the quickest road to distance casting is to learn to cast 40 feet of line effortlessly. Once you get things down pat, you can start working on your distance. It is definitely a mistake to get too fancy too soon.

As I said in the last chapter, I think the best way to learn to cast is to keep your elbow pretty much at your side unless you have good reason for bringing it up. Learning in this manner helps to stop the rod overhead; if you hold the elbow down and keep the wrist stiff, you've got to stop the rod correctly. But for distance casting you may want to get a longer drive stroke, and there are other occasions when you need to raise the elbow considerably.

There is a way to increase the total rod-forward movement without increasing the arc. The trick is to raise your elbow up and out. Then you drive the whole rod straight ahead. The best illustration I've seen of this principle appeared in a booklet by Scientific Anglers, and I have obtained permission to reprint it here. Note that the hand and the entire rod move forward, and the direction of applied force is al-

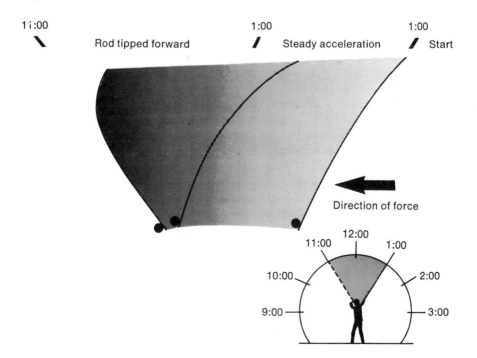

most in a straight line. You simply raise your elbow on the backcast, pause for the line tug, and drive the rod forward and straight ahead; then you tip the rod forward sharply with a wrist movement and thumb pressure. Note carefully that the arc described by the rod is still from 1 o'clock to 11—although the "clock dial" itself moves forward. During the movement from A to B, the rod remains cocked in the 1 o'clock position. What this movement does is increase the length of the power stroke while keeping the arc narrow and the loop tight.

I might add that Scientific Anglers recommended this cast as standard, whether you want to cast 30 feet or 100. Further, they recommended that you start casting with this basic procedure. A good argument might be made for this, and the angler could do a good deal worse. But, personally, I find this cast more tiring for normal distances than the old "elbow at the side" cast. I also have trouble holding the rod vertical and then tipping it with wrist movement. So, when I use this method, I usually start the arc and continue it during the entire stroke. But this is the sort of thing that each angler should work out for himself as he gains experience.

No matter whether you move the elbow or keep it put, you can definitely increase line speed by stopping sharply at the end of the power stroke, both on the backcast and on the forward cast. Emphatically stopping the rod causes the tip to spring forward (or back on the backcast), thereby unloading the rod. If you don't take advantage of the energy stored in the rod, then you are, at least in part, slinging the line out instead of casting it fully. The same thing is true of casting with spinning or baitcasting rods, and, I might add, most anglers do tend to sling either a lure or a fly line. Although they can surely catch bass by so doing, they are just making it harder on themselves.

In addition to making full use of the stop, some experts go a step farther with a wrist flick and thumb pressure at the end of the forward power stroke. This is difficult to describe, but I would call it a sort of double-clutching movement. What they do is stop the rod arm, then emphasize the tip movement with the wrist and thumb. Still other anglers tip the rod *back* a bit after making the stop and before releasing the shooting line; this backward tip apparently accelerates the forming of the loop and keeps it tighter.

Although good casting form and habits together with a few tricks will enable the angler to cast long distances, the best way to increase line speed is to use line hauls. Normally, the line hand more or less follows the rod hand, and its function is to maintain tension on the line. When making a haul, the line hand not only maintains the necessary tension but also pulls the line. Although most fly-rodders with any experience will use a line haul of sorts on the pickup and backcast, the principle is fully realized only in the double haul. It is not easy. It requires study, concentration, good timing, and practice.

The double haul is primarily an aid to distance casting, and it really isn't required unless you want to make very long casts. The bass angler, however, can use hauls to advantage when casting heavy bugs for shorter distances, and I find a double haul to be especially useful for casting bugs into a strong head wind. I therefore recommend that the bass angler learn how to make hauls and that he practice them during his routine fishing, just to get the timing down pat.

Personally, I almost always make a single haul of sorts when I am casting with a fly rod. On the pickup, the line hand grasps the line near the stripping guide. As the rod hand is raised, the line hand hauls down. This aids in the pickup simply because it helps get the line moving. And it speeds up the line during the power stroke of the backcast. So far this is pretty simple, and I think that most anglers who do a lot of fly casting make some sort of single haul on the pickup, whether or not they realize it. This is especially true of anglers who work a shoreline or otherwise make repeated casts.

Anyhow, the double haul starts with a relatively simple single haul on the pickup. Assume that the angler pulled in a yard of line with the single haul. As soon as he completes the power stroke of the backcast, and while drifting the rod back, he feeds this yard of line, while maintaining a slight tension on it, back through the rod guides. His line hand sort of follows the rod and may extend almost to the stripping guide. The fly line, of course, is straightening out behind the angler, so that feeding the line is not difficult once one has mastered the timing. The beginner should watch his backcast over his shoulder so that he'll get a better feeling for what's going on. A high, fast backcast will help things go smoothly.

After the angler has fed the line through the rod guides, he brings the rod forward and hauls the line back down. The rod hand stops the forward stroke and the line hand drops the line. The rod drifts down and the running line shoots through the guides. (Some anglers try not to release the shooting line until they feel a slight forward

STOP ROD

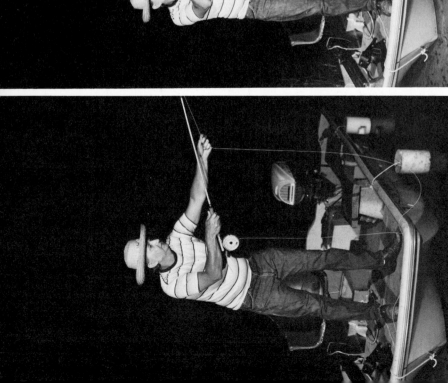

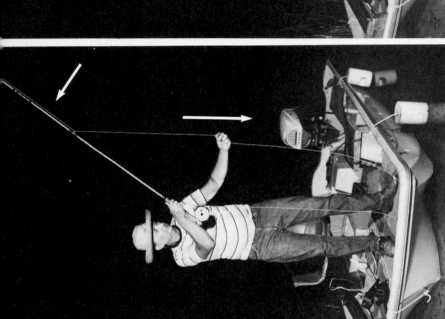

When the rod is stopped, the line hand has hauled quite a length of line down. In an actual cast, the line hand would be behind the angler's hip pocket.

Bring the rod up for the power stroke and haul the line down with the line hand.

Start the double haul by grasping the line out in front of you.

DRIFT

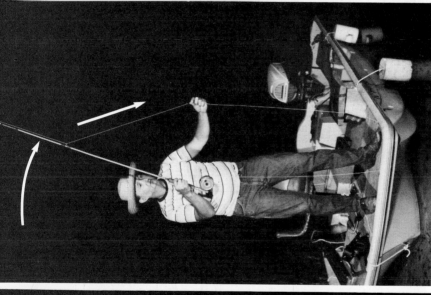

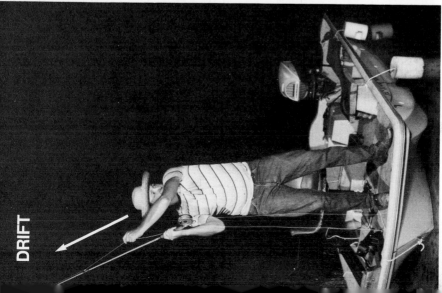

DRIFT

After the power stroke for the forward cast has been completed, the angler releases line for shooting.

After the backcast has straightened out and the angler has fed out the line, he starts a forceful forward cast and hauls the line down sharply.

While the rod is drifting back during the pause, the line hand feeds the line through the rod guides.

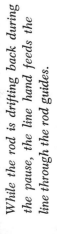

tug; others drop the line immediately on completing the forward power stroke.)

It might seem ridiculous to haul in line with your line hand when you are trying to cast it out with your rod hand, but the purpose of the haul is to increase the line speed. If things work right, you can shoot out much more line than you hauled in. The greater the line speed, the more distance you can get when shooting.

There is a good bit of leeway on the distance and the intensity of the haul. It might be merely a tug on the line, or, if the angler is shooting for distance, he might haul the line forcefully for almost 6 feet, ending up with his line hand back beyond his hip pocket! If photographed at the right time, some distance experts would look more like discus throwers than fly casters!

I almost have to add that many distance casters disregard the classic clock-dial casting directions, and certainly don't hold the 12 and 1 o'clock positions as sacred. Some of them let the rod drift back almost horizontally. For other points of view, see *Fly Casting with Lefty Kreh, Fly Casting with Bill Cairns,* Charles Ritz's *A Fly Fisher's Life,* and Jim Green's *Fly Casting.*

A specialist at distance shooting can work out 30 feet of shooting taper and then get out a total of 100 feet in short order. The problem is what to do with the 70 feet of running line—how to keep it from tangling, how to get it through the guides properly, and how to keep it ready to shoot at all times. If you are on a boat with a casting deck, you can carefully coil the line before you make the cast, or, if you are wading, you can carefully put it into a stripping basket. Some anglers even loop it over some sort of clip on their waders, or hold coils in their mouth. All this is fine for the angler who doesn't make fast, repeated casts. He can coil his line ahead of time and be ready. But the bassman needs to keep his bug in the water, and all that line just gets in the way.

In short, I don't think that shooting heads and long running lines are practical for bass fishing. The exceptions might include jump fishing and the use of lead-core shooting heads for fishing structure in deep water.

Anyhow, if you plan to do a lot of distance shooting, you'll need to work out some method of holding the line coiled properly.

Wind causes some problems for the fly caster, and a lot of anglers either quit fishing or look for secluded spots when the going gets a little rough. No one can fish in a hurricane, but normal wind speeds up to 20 miles an hour can be overcome, and, in fact, bass fishing is often better when there is some chop on the water. My personal policy is to fish where I think the bass are *if* my electric fishing motor will handle the boat. In other words, it's boat-handling problems, not wind-related casting problems, that cause me to quit a hot spot. I do, however, usually make shorter casts in a stiff breeze. For one thing, the bass can't see the angler or his boat as readily if there is some chop on the water.

One way to beat the wind is to keep your cast low. Wind speeds will often be greater a few feet above your head, especially if you are fishing along a wooded shoreline. Regular overhead casts can be made in wind, but, in most cases, it's best to keep your line low and your loop tight. Making a side cast (discussed in the next chapter) will help, and it is often possible to make a horizontal side cast in which rod and line get only a few feet off the water. Side casts are, however, rather limited on distance, and it's difficult for two anglers to make side casts off the same boat.

Another way to beat the wind is to increase the line speed by any of the methods discussed earlier in this chapter. Note also that the weight and wind resistance of a bug or fly has a bearing on line speed, and often merely changing lures will solve some casting problems.

If I have a choice, I prefer to cast into head winds instead of casting with tail winds. A tail wind makes the backcast awkward and complicates the angler's timing; the wind impedes the backcast so that the line doesn't load the rod properly, making it difficult to detect the little tug that signals the angler to proceed with the forward cast. A head wind, on the other hand, helps the backcast and emphasizes the line tug at the end of the pause. After you have a good backcast going for you, it is fairly easy to drive even a bass bug into a stiff head wind, provided that your gear is heavy enough and is reasonably matched. Making a line haul on the forward stroke helps a lot when you are driving a bug into a head wind. In any case, casting into a head wind causes no timing problems, and all the angler has to learn is how to drive the bug.

Generally, it is best to keep the backcast high and the forward cast low. Keeping the backcast up puts the wind to good use, and keeping the forward cast low will, at least at times, put the bug down under the stronger winds. Such a cast will, however, tend to splat the bug down onto the water instead of presenting it gently. But a gentle presentation isn't too important when there is some chop on the water.

A strong head wind can cause some problems when you are trying to shoot for distance. The best bet is to increase line speed and keep the forward cast low with a very tight loop; don't release the shooting line until the rod has drifted down almost to the horizontal position.

When casting with a tail wind, remember that your backcast will have to be made into the wind; consequently, it is highly desirable to keep the backcast low. And fast. A low backcast, however, together with the tail wind, causes the line and fly to return too close to the angler on the forward cast, and more than one fly-rodder has wrapped the line around himself in a stiff tail wind. The best bet is to make the backcast with the rod at about a 45-degree angle from the vertical; in other words, make the backcast with a modified side cast. This keeps the line lower while at the same time permitting a shallow loop. After making such a backcast, bring the rod to vertical (during the pause) and make a high forward cast. The reason for making a high forward cast is to put the line up into the wind so that it will help the cast. Such a "floating" cast isn't quite as accurate as a normal cast, however. But it is probably the best way to cope with a strong tail wind. Speeding up the backcast with a line haul and some muscle will help.

Finally, you might try facing the wind, making a false cast into it, and then fishing on your "backcast." This method will often work if great accuracy isn't required.

A crosswind that blows the line away from the angler doesn't cause too much of a problem. If you cast with your right hand, such a wind would be blowing in from your left (or the reverse for south-paws). Distance and accuracy may be impaired, but such a cross-wind can usually be allowed for.

An adverse crosswind is another matter. I'm talking about a wind that tends to blow the line and lure back into the angler. If you are right-handed, a wind blowing in strong from your right will catch the line and cause the fly or bug to zip past dangerously close to your ear. It is very important that the angler watch his business and some-how keep the line downwind. A backhand cast will work. Or the angler might make an overhead cast by raising his casting arm high for the backcast, then letting his arm drift down a little to the left during the pause. When the power stroke is made, the line and lure come by on the angler's left. In other words, the fly comes by the angler on the right on the backcast, and returns on his left during the forward cast. Personally, however, I've never cared much for this cast, and I would just as soon have a bug in my right ear as in my left.

The best bet is to avoid steady casting in this type of crosswind. Most bass anglers fishing from boats with bow-mounted electric motors can merely change directions, thereby putting the crosswind to the other side. Instead of fishing down a shoreline, fish up it, or vice versa. Why fight a crosswind for two or three hours? Anglers fishing on streams will have to live with crosswinds at times, but most bass streams bend around and offer good fishing on either side, so that the angler isn't continuously fighting an adverse crosswind. Besides, wind isn't usually as much of a problem on bass streams as it is on a large lake or impoundment.

I would like to emphasize that large, wind-resistant bass bugs are dangerous, with or without winds. I didn't realize just how dangerous until my daughter had a bug stick in her eye. Fortunately, the hook merely buried up under the lid and didn't penetrate the eyeball—but we didn't know that during the long ride back to the boat landing and during the 22-mile drive to the nearest hospital emergency room. We were lucky.

15

Fishing Streams and Tight Places

MOST OF THE INFORMATION in Part Three, on when and where to catch bass, will apply to fishing in large streams and small. Oxygen content, temperature, wind, and so on aren't quite as variable on streams as they are on large lakes and impoundments, and therefore aren't normally as much of a factor to be reckoned with. But bass in a stream prefer cover and shade just as surely as they do anywhere else. Stumps, logs, pockets, run-ins, and so on are just as important in streams as they are in natural lakes and impoundments. So is deep water, and the larger bass will often be in or near deep holes.

One difference with stream bass, however, is that the current is another factor in their choice of feeding or holding areas. Bass in streams are fond of hanging out in eddies near swift water, say, behind a boulder at the end of a shoal run. In general, however, bass don't hang out in really swift water. But any change in flow, such as an eddy hole, should be fished out thoroughly. The interface between fast water and slow should also be fished. And always remember that bass will usually be facing the current, and place your casts accordingly.

Wading shallow streams can be a most enjoyable form of fly-fishing. This angler is wading the Hillsborough River in Florida.

The big difference in fly-rodding for bass on a stream is primarily a matter of mechanics. Casting is more difficult on some streams because of trees along the bank, and the current working against the large fly line causes problems in fishing a bug, streamer, or other lure properly. Here are some tricks that will help:

The roll cast. Often on streams, and sometimes on lakes, you won't have enough room behind you to make a backcast. The roll cast will usually work, since it doesn't require any backcast at all. Although it isn't great for distance or accuracy, you can, after a few practice casts, get a bug out 40 feet or so, and practice will improve your accuracy. I recommend that you make a roll cast from time to time even when you don't need it.

Proceed by raising the rod slowly to the 12:30 position. Pause briefly, then drive the rod with an accelerating motion to 10 o'clock. Stop. Emphasize the stop. Then let the rod drift down nearly to vertical.

If you want a little more distance on a roll cast, you can shoot some line immediately after the stop. Or you can work out a little line when you are raising the rod tip to 12:30, but remember that the line must not be allowed to go slack.

Typically, a roll cast presents the lure gently enough. Note, however, that controlling the loop will permit some variation. The loop is controlled by the arc of the power stroke. A wide arc results in a deep loop; a narrow arc, in a shallow loop. If you stop the rod at 10:30, the line will roll in the air. If you apply a wide arc and stop

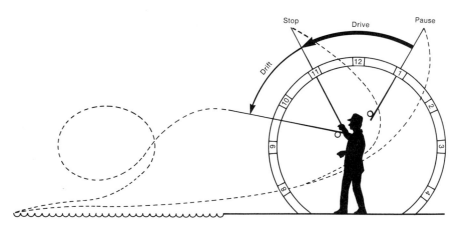

The roll cast.

at 9:30, the line will roll on the water. Keeping the arc narrow and stopping at 10:00 will be about right. If you want the line to unroll higher above the water, start the power stroke at 1:00 or 1:30 and stop it at 10:30 or 11:00 and hold back somewhat on the drift.

You can make roll casts with sinking line and light streamers or bucktails as well as with floating lines and bugs. The procedure is pretty much the same, except maybe for raising the rod tip a little faster when you're getting ready to cast a sinking line.

A roll can also be used at times to unsnag a bug or fly, and a roll pickup can often be used to help get a lure out of grass and thick cover. Some anglers also use a roll to get a sinking line up near the surface, then proceed with a regular pickup.

Steeple cast. Often there will be too much obstruction behind you for a normal cast, but not enough to require a roll cast. If you use your full arm and make a quick pickup, emphasizing an upward thrust, you can throw the fly line almost straight up. Then start the

The author watches a high backcast on a small stream.

forward cast without much of a pause. Actually, the forward cast requires very little power; instead, the rod is used to sort of direct the downward fall of the line. If you do make a powerful forward stroke, your line and bug will spat down into the water heavily. Instead of a power stroke, try dropping the arm down and drifting the rod forward.

Pocket cast. It's always a good idea to know what's behind you when you're fishing a stream or other tight spots. One trick that often works is to find an opening in the trees behind you and cast to it. This can be done by looking over your shoulder on the backcast, or even by facing the pocket, casting to it, and presenting the lure on the "backcast."

Flop cast. When I am drifting down a small stream on a boat or tube, or proceeding upstream with the aid of an electric motor, I'll often merely flop the lure from one side of the boat to the other. Typically, I'll fish the lure for only 2 or 3 feet before flopping it over to the other side. I've gone for a mile or more up or down a bushy stream without making a single backcast! The flop cast can be made from overhead or from the side. I usually hold my rod forward off the bow of the boat and flick the lure from one bank to the other. This technique works best in rather sluggish streams averaging from 50 to 60 feet across. The boat, of course, should be kept in midstream.

Side cast. Here's a cast that can be used when there is no space for an overhead cast, for example, when you are standing under a tree. Use the regular casting cycle, but simply hold the rod at a angle instead of vertical. I often use a horizontal side cast to get bugs and flies under overhanging brush. It's also a useful cast to make in high wind, but it is rather limited in distance.

Backhand cast. This cast can be made by holding the rod at some angle across your body. The angle can vary from almost vertical to almost horizontal. The backhand cast can be used in wind, or when obstructions make an overhead cast impossible.

Curve cast. A curve cast, made from one side or the other, can be helpful in current, so that line mending can be held to a minimum. The object is to have the line curving upstream, making a reverse belly; then the line, being caught in the current, won't as quickly pull your bug or fly out of position. A curve cast also helps the angler get a bug back behind stumps and other cover, or into pockets that would be inaccessible by a regular overhead forward cast.

The best text I've seen on the curve cast appeared in *Fly Casting with Bill Cairns,* and I have obtained permission to quote it here at some length:

> The easiest way to throw these curves is to operate from the side. You will recall that our basic cast can come from any angle and no matter what the point of origin is. If it is a well-timed delivery, the result is a straight line. Recognizing this, we see that if we cast side-arm the line loops form roughly parallel to the water and a properly timed cast will straighten out in front of us. But an underpowered side cast will fail to attain the straight line; it will fall in a negative curve. Conversely, an overpowered side cast will extend the leader and fly past the straight line and result in a positive curve.
>
> The negative curve is probably the easiest to start with. In fact, with a short line just underpower your usual side cast stroke and you'll see the principle very quickly.
>
> If the cast is straightening out, too much power is being applied. It may take several tries to hit it right since the unconscious tendency is to try and throw a normal straightline extension. What you are trying to accomplish is a premature arrival of the line on the water. This takes very little power to achieve.
>
> At longer casting distances loop or hold several feet of excess slack in the line hand. Make a horizontal pickup and backcast. Keep the motions slightly underpowered using the middle of the rod without any final tip-action input. After the backcast straightens, bring the rod forward again, slightly underpowered, using the middle of the rod without the usual thumb and wrist pressure acceleration. Before the line loop straightens, release the slack from the line-holding hand. This premature release of the slack stops the loop from completing itself and straightening out. Properly done, the line falls in a negative curve on the water.
>
> In effect, this negative curve is the opposite of everything we normally try to do. It is an incomplete, underpowered cast in every respect.
>
> To some degree the amount of potential curve is controlled by the rod angle when casting. The true sidearm cast can throw the deepest curve. A higher rod angle permits less of a curve.
>
> The positive curve differs in execution in that we shall overpower the cast. The side cast is again used as the basis of the cast's formation. Start with the horizontal pickup and backcast using unnatural motion with the final wrist and thumb impetus to keep a neat, narrow loop. After the backcast straightens start the forward stroke with more power than would be needed to

simply straighten the line. Finish with a forceful wrist and thumb pressure application. A short line hand pull just as the thumb pressure is applied will help "throw the tip in." At the finish of the cast stop the rod abruptly and raise the rod tip slightly. This overpowered motion will cause the leader and fly to swing past their normal straight line. The leader and fly will turn into a positive curve on the water.

Curves can also be done easily with backhand casting strokes. This can be valuable if you're hemmed in on the casting arm side by foliage. A lazy backhand cast will make the negative curve; a forceful backhand cast, aided by the line hand tug, will kick into a positive curve.

Line mending. The current in a stream can cause some pretty severe problems at times. Assume, for example, that you make a cast across the stream to a likely-looking eddy hole. Your bug lands just right, and you want to fish the hole with a very slow, twitch-and-rest motion. But the current will be likely to catch your fly line, which will quickly form a belly and create a drag on your bug. In short, the line will pull the bug out of the hole you want to fish. Line mending will sometimes help you keep the bug in position a little longer.

The trick is simply to hold the rod out in front of you and roll it upstream. The roll is made with the forearm, and the wrist is held stiff. The difficult thing is controlling the roll so that you don't yourself pull the bug out of position, and I personally find this hard to do.

The best bet is to first make a curve cast, and then mend the line as necessary. The curve cast will permit you to lay an upstream belly in the line, and as soon as the current moves the belly downstream and starts to drag the bug, simply roll the belly back upstream.

Most anglers who fish streams with a boat or tube merely drift with the current, simply because drifting or floating is the easiest way to go. Floating from one bridge or access point to another is by far the most popular way to fish some streams. If you want to slow the boat down, get about 5 feet of heavy chain and tie it to a line. Then drag it like an anchor. The boat's speed can be adjusted by letting out or taking in more line. Letting out line will slow the boat down; taking in line will speed it up. The chain will occasionally hang up on the bottom, but it will usually snake over or through surprisingly thick log jams, rocks, and other debris. I do, however, have reservations about dragging a chain over a hard bottom because I believe it may make undesirable sounds, which carry for long distances downstream.

Anglers who have foot-controlled motors on their boat, as well as those who prefer manual electric motors, have a choice of fishing upstream or down if the motor is powerful enough to pull the boat against the current. Anglers who wade also have a choice. In some cases, however, it would be impractical to proceed upstream, as when the boater must face swift water and would too quickly run down his battery or when the tube fisherman is on a stream with deep holes and impassable banks. But it is almost always better to fish upstream if you can do so without too much difficulty. The reasons are several:

1. Bass almost invariably face upstream, simply because food drifts with the current. Since they are facing upstream, they are less likely to see you if you approach from downstream.

2. Bass are more likely to see your lure if it is retrieved with the current instead of against it. Assume, for example, that a bass is waylaying beside a stump. If you cast downstream and retrieve upstream, the bass won't see the lure approach. It will come from behind, and might even spook the bass. If you cast upstream, however, the bass will see the lure hit the water and will watch it approach. Besides, a bug or fly looks more natural if it is caught in the current.

3. Sounds and vibrations made by wading or bumping things around in a boat carry much farther downstream than they do upstream.

4. Anything that bass can taste or smell carries downstream. There is pretty good evidence that a hooked or wounded fish exudes some chemical substance that warns others of its kind of danger, and I believe that this substance can spook bass downstream from you. I've read that an angler merely washing his hands in a stream can have a bad effect on salmon fishing for several miles downstream. I doubt that bass are that sensitive to smells and tastes, but, on the other hand, I think that the angler should have respect for the senses of any fish. One of my nephews is the best creek angler I know, and he won't spit tobacco juice into the water if he is proceeding downstream!

Most of the lures discussed in Part Two can be used on a stream, but the mechanics of fishing them are a little different than on an impoundment or a lake. A popping bug won't often be dead in a stream as it will be on a lake; it will drift with the current. The angler will therefore have to vary his retrieve to suit the occasion. The current will often be something of a problem, but, on the other hand, the angler can just as often use the current to his advantage. He can, for example, cast ahead of a likely bass spot, then float his bug into position. Sometimes a lure can be held just out of a treetop or log or some such cover with excellent results, and a bug can be floated under overhanging brush. And merely following the natural drift of the current is sometimes the best possible way to work streamers and bucktails. I might add that some anglers tend to overwork lures in current, and this is especially true of streamers and bucktails; the current itself imparts movement to the lure as a whole as well as to the feathers and hair. So use the current to your advantage instead of fighting it.

A spinner and weighted fly can often be deadly on a stream. My favorite combination is a large weighted Wooly Worm with a suitable Colorado spinner and a pork trailer about 1½ times as long as the fly. In shallow streams, I do retrieve this rig by stripping in line, but in deep water the trick is to cast across the current or slightly into it. Hold the line tight while the weighted fly sinks down along a bank or some likely bass haunt. After it sinks down near the bottom, you can of course start a retrieve—but 90 percent of your strikes will occur while the lure sinks. I know a master of this technique who will bet a nickel on every cast on his favorite stream (clear and deep) at the right time of the year. And he almost broke me. Try it.

16

Hooking
and
Playing Bass

ANY ANGLER IS GOING to miss some strikes and is going to lose a hooked bass from time to time. But some anglers do connect on a higher percentage of their strikes, and I seem to be one of these. On more than one fishing trip, I have landed more bass than companions who were better casters than I, who seemed to work harder, and who got more strikes. Although it is true that some anglers are naturally faster than others, anyone can raise his average by giving some thought to the matter. Consider:

Slack line. My guess is that more bass are missed because of slack line than for any other single reason. Slack line delays the strike —and anyone who has ever watched a bass suck in and spit out a lure knows that a fraction of a second can be important. Slack line also wastes some (or even all) of the rod's strike arc simply because the angler doesn't get a direct pull on the fish until the slack line is taken up. That is not entirely accurate, however, because the drag of the line in the water will often set the hook, and the large-diameter fly lines have more drag and surface tension than lines used on spinning or baitcasting gear.

Being alert and having your gear shipshape often make the difference be-
tween catching fish and merely getting a few strikes. This nice stringer of
bass and panfish was taken with a fly rod in North Carolina.

To some extent, slack is inevitable when the angler is fishing in a stream because the current makes a belly in the line. The same problem—a belly—occurs when you are casting bugs and other slow lures to a bank ahead of a moving boat. It is impossible to eliminate slack line when fishing a bug properly, but it can be regulated somewhat by stripping in line or, possibly, by mending the line. The problem here is to get the slack out of the line without pulling the bug out of position.

In any case, it pays to be aware of slack line so that you'll be ready to set the hook harder and with a wide strike arc. It will also help to make a long, quick haul with your line hand when you attempt to set the hook with a lot of slack line out.

Tight-line retrieves. There are several ways to work and retrieve a bug or fly, and too many anglers err by always using the rod tip. It is, of course, sometimes desirable to twitch bugs and flies with the rod tip, or to lift some lures with a long, upward sweep of the rod. Most of the time, however, the bass angler will profit by keeping his rod tip down, pointed directly toward the lure. Having the rod horizontal and ready has obvious advantages when setting the hook.

There are two basic retrieves which permit the angler to work the lure with little or no rod action and which can be used to work in slack.

The first is to strip in line, making hauls of from a few inches to a few feet. This is a good stop-and-go retrieve, and, by pulling smartly on the line, the angler can even make a popping bug do its thing. To make this retrieve, hold the line with the index and middle finger of the rod hand, as shown in the accompanying photograph, and

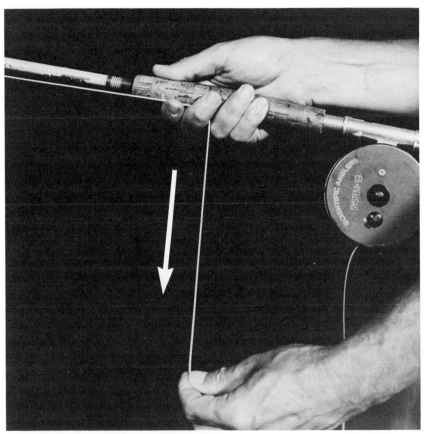

Stripping retrieve. The author holds the line under two rod-hand fingers because it gives him a better grip on the line, but many anglers use only the index finger.

strip in line with the other hand. By using both hands, the angler is always in touch with his line and is ready to strike at any time.

The second is the hand-twist retrieve. It is good for taking in slack line and for moving the lure with a slow, steady motion. The hand-twist is illustrated in the accompanying photographs.

Whichever way you choose to make a retrieve, it is very important that you *always* keep a firm grip on your fly line. Be ready to respond to a strike at any time. Far too many bass have been missed because the angler dropped the line in order to reach for a pack of cigarettes or to scratch a mosquito bite. Always secure the line under the index and middle fingers of the rod hand before relieving your line hand of its duty. By the way, if bass seem to be psychic in knowing exactly when the angler drops his line and strike accordingly, it is probably because the angler at such times lets his bug rest longer than usual or lets his streamer sink deeper.

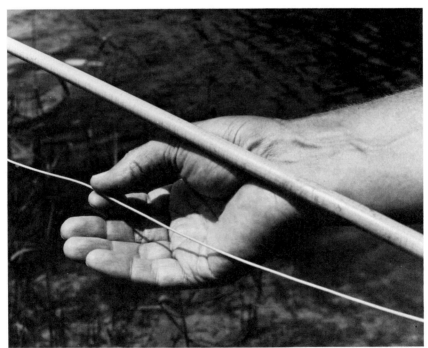

To make the hand-twist retrieve, grasp the line under the rod with your thumb and forefinger.

Turn your hand and gather in the line with your fingers while maintaining the thumb and forefinger grip.

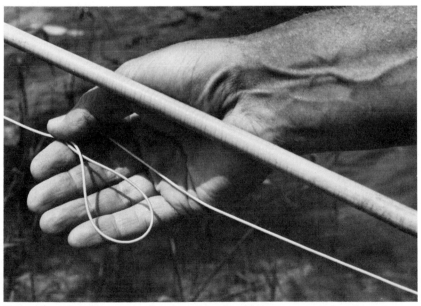

Turn your hand again and grasp more line between your thumb and forefinger. Repeat this procedure throughout the retrieve.

The back-snap. Anglers who set the hook with a quick snap or jerk instead of a pull should be aware of what I call the rod's back-snap, a phenomenon that occurs with all rods but which is more severe in fiberglass (as compared to bamboo or graphite) and is usually more pronounced in long, limber fly rods. The back-snap can delay the strike for a fraction of a second and cause the tippet to break from impact. Here's an explanation from Charles Waterman's *Modern Fresh and Salt Water Fly Fishing:*

> Before the happy business of subduing the fish, the hook must be set, and the motion is best described as a quick lift of the tip. In other efforts, there may be little difference between a "quick lift" and a "jerk," but there is when a fly rod is involved. The catch is that when a fly rod is jerked quickly and hard, the tip bends toward the fish before it starts moving the other way. This means that instead of taking up slack instantly, the tip actually gives the fish more slack momentarily. Then, as the fisherman's strike is continued, the tip springs back, tightening the line and going with the fisherman's yank, placing a heavy strain on the leader. Not only is it easy to break light tippets this way, but the angler's too sudden strike actually gives a fast fish more time to discard the fly than if the move has been a sharp lift.
>
> The physics of this business is nothing earthshaking. Just hold a rod a few inches above the horizontal to a table, and jerk upward. The tip will flick down and hit the table before following the motion of the rest of the rod. Now, or course, many of us get a little jerk into our lift and the rod may dip a little before coming up, but experienced fishermen learn to keep it to a minimum, and the "quick lift" or "quick sweep" is very different from the jerk.

Be alert. The angler who watches his business will catch more bass than one who daydreams. Always expect a strike. It helps to keep your eye on a bug or surface lure, and if the bass don't seem to mind, I often choose a bug that *I* can see, such as fluorescent red or chartreuse. When fishing streamers or other sinking lures, watch your fly line. Any twitch or movement can indicate that a bass has your lure. Think of your fly line as a visual indicator. It is, in fact, a very good one, and is more sensitive than bulky floats.

Sharp hooks. In all fishing, it is important that the angler's hook be sharp. This is especially true when one is using large bugs and saltwater flies. Heavy-duty hooks in sizes larger than 3/0 will pene-

Keeping your hooks sharp will improve your catch, especially with large bugs and streamers. The author uses either a small file or a whetstone.

trate better if the angler will take the trouble to triangulate the point with a file, so that it will have three cutting edges.

Setting the hook. It's not necessary to jerk as hard as plastic-worm fishermen do, but you must remember to set the hook with authority. Then quickly lower the rod tip, strip in slack line, and set it again.

Just as some anglers will connect on a larger percentage of their strikes than their companions will, still others will actually boat or land more bass after hooking them. Experience will help give the angler confidence in this matter and will, or should, help him stay cool during the battle, but after landing thousands of bass and not a few lunkers I hesitate to give anyone advice. Shortly after I was married, my wife and I were fishing one calm afternoon when she tied into a large bass. The thing came out from under an overhanging brush top and hit within 10 feet of the boat. She quickly horsed it within arm's reach and was about, it seemed, to lift it out of the water. Well, that might well have been the thing to do; she might well have got the bass into the boat before it knew what was going on. But I doubted that her 10-pound line would take the strain, and I started yelling at her to give it quarter. The bass hadn't even begun to fight. Anyhow, it got loose pretty quick, and, looking back, I doubt that it was hooked solidly.

She had not yet caught a large bass, and she was upset about the thing. "You should have grabbed it, or something," she said, "when I had it at the boat."

Well, I might possibly have netted the fish or "grabbed it," but I still think that I gave her the right advice. This story is a little complicated by the fact that I caught "her" fish (or an 8-pounder from under the same brush) the next day. I will say only that I advised her in good conscience, and I offer the following considerations in the same spirit:

1. Most fly-rodders, including myself, work a fish in by stripping line. The procedure is similar to a regular stripping retrieve. Some experts, however, advise the angler to use the fly reel to bring in fish. One reason is that you'll need to use the reel if you ever go after big game, such as tarpon. To be sure, the angler can land bass by stripping in line, but the point is that he may be developing a bad habit that he'll later regret. I might add that I don't regret it. I feel that I can always resort to the reel after a fish has taken all my working line.

2. As everyone knows, the best way to whip a fish down is to hold the rod at a rather high angle, so that the rod will do its thing. I believe that 45 degrees is about right. But the angler should know that he can increase or decrease his effective drag merely by raising or lowering the rod. The higher the rod, the greater the drag caused by friction as the line goes over the rod guides and tip.

3. Holding the rod high, or low, can help you get a bass out of thick cover. In grass, for example, you can sometimes keep a bass from digging in by standing up and holding the rod high over your head. The same high position will help you get a fish over a submerged log if the fish is behind the log (on the far side). If the fish has gone under the log from the near side, however, you'll be trying

to bring it under instead of over the log, in which case you should hold the rod as low as possible. You can even stick it down into the water.

4. One problem is what to do when a hooked fish runs toward the angler. It is, of course, more likely to get off if it has slack line. The only thing I know is to take in the slack as quickly as possible. I normally do this by stripping in line, but the reel may be used unless the angler has coils of surplus line off the reel. An automatic reel is very good in this situation, but it has limitations and disadvantages that in my opinion outweigh this advantage.

5. Often a large bass will run under the boat, where it may foul the line on the electric or outboard shafts or props. The best bet is to stick the rod down into the water and either try to bring the bass back to your side of the boat or else try to work the rod around either end of the boat. I usually prefer the latter if I have a big fish on and it has gone all the way to the other side of the boat. If at all possible, however, it is better to avoid this situation in the first place. It helps to use the electric motor to swing the bow of the boat one way or the other. Just don't cut your line with the electric's prop. Personally, I tilt the kicker out of the water before I start fishing, unless I have good reason to leave it down.

6. Anchor lines in the water have caused the bassman to lose some real lunkers. If two anglers are aboard a boat, one can get the anchor up as soon as his companion ties into a trophy bass. If you are fishing alone, drop only the stern anchor and keep the bow-mounted electric in the water; then try to maneuver the boat so that you can avoid the anchor line. I also like the new push-button electric anchors. I might add that there is seldom any need to anchor if you are fishing in shallow water and have a good bow-mounted electric motor on your boat. In fact, it's usually best to keep moving unless you have good reason to stop at a certain spot.

7. If you tie into a lunker bass and have enough open water to let it run, take a quick glance at the surplus line that may be coiled at your feet. If it is wrapped around the electric's foot pedal or something, try to free it before things get hectic. The best bet, however, is to keep your line tidy *before* you tie into that lunker. It also pays to keep the "memory coils" out of your line as much as possible. Stretching the line from time to time will help, and it also helps to have a reel with a large-diameter spool.

8. There are two schools of thought on what to do when a bass

jumps, and both are at least partly correct. Some anglers say to point your rod at the fish, thereby giving slack; if you don't give slack, the bass may break your line, what with all that violent headshaking. Others say to keep the line tight, lower the rod, and try to force the fish back down into the water; if you do give slack, they say, the bass is more likely to shake your lure out of its mouth. In my opinion, there is no single method that works best with all kinds of fishing.

If I'm using a heavy plug or jig with a 20-pound test line, I'll keep my line tight. The heavy line is likely to stand up, and slack line permits the bass to shake the plug or jig too freely. All that weight slinging around can indeed pull the hook out. But with a fly rod and a bug and, say, an 8-pound tippet, it is probably better to give slack by pointing the rod directly at the bass. A bug or fly is very light as compared to baitcasting hardware so that the bass isn't as likely to throw it. And trying to horse the bass down during all that frantic movement could well put too much strain on the tippet. Besides, I like to see a fish jump freely.

While taking a break from writing this chapter, I went out to fish for 30 minutes or so and hooked three bass on a rubber spider. The thing was attached to a spinner shaft that had a keel-weighted head, and I was casting it with a spinning outfit. This is in my opinion the worst sort of lure on which to land a bass. The weight is concentrated a good ways from the bend of the hook and is connected to the hook eyelet with a wire loop, which permits the weight to flop about. Anyhow, I lost all three bass on jumps. If I had removed all that hardware and used the spider on my fly rod, I would have probably landed all three. In my opinion, a light fly and a long, limber rod are the best possible combination for landing fish, unless you are fishing in a submerged jungle.

9. One of the worst mistakes you can make with a lunker bass or other large fish is to take in too much line toward the end of the battle. Never—I mean *never*—bring the leader into the rod tip and guides. If the knot gets caught, as it very often will, and the fish makes a last-effort lunge, you'll be likely to lose it, especially with a light tippet. Once your leader gets caught, there's really nothing you can do, since you can't reach out to the end of the fly rod during the critical moment. Smooth knots and ring guides will help—but this problem is easily avoided in the first place by watching what you are doing.

10. If you have a heavy fish on, it's best to work the fish in by pumping the rod. The trick is to hold the line tight while raising the rod slowly. Then lower the rod slowly while you gain line either with your line hand or with your reel. Repeat the process until you have the fish in. Such a retrieve maintains a more constant pressure and gives the angler a better feeling for what the fish is doing.

11. As I stated in Chapter 4, the best way to land a large bass is to grip it by the lower jaw with the thumb and forefinger of your line hand. A lot of anglers, however, do prefer to use a net, for one reason or another. If you are one of these, be sure to get a net that's large enough for lunkers and learn how to use it. Always net a fish headfirst. Swooping at it from the rear is definitely a mistake. The best procedure is to lower the net, at an angle, into the water and then bring the bass over it. During the final moments of the battle, the net is perfectly still until the bass is over it. Then the net is simply lifted up.

In my opinion, it is best to exhaust a bass before attempting to net it. But some experts and bass pros want to bring the fish in as quickly as possible. The saying is that the time to play with a bass is after you have it in the boat. At times, as in heavy cover, it is indeed better to get the fish in as quickly as possible, before it wraps around something and breaks off. And there may be other valid reasons for bringing a fish on in. One of the bass pros told me that he didn't have time to play a fish down.

Another consideration along this line is that there is pretty good evidence that a hooked fish will spook any other bass in the immediate area; consequently, the quicker you get a bass out of the water the better are your chances of catching another one nearby. I think there might well be something in this, but, personally, I'm going to play an 8-pound bass pretty well if the water is open. My thinking is that one lunker in the hand is worth two in the water.

12. Finally, the best advice I can give is this: Be sure that your tippet stays in good shape. Inspect it frequently for abrasion and wind knots. I lost a 5-pound bass just a week or two ago by pure negligence in this respect. I was fishing for bluegills with a No. 8 bug when I tied into the bass, and I just wasn't expecting such a large fish on so small a lure. After it broke off, inspection showed that I had a wind knot in my 6-pound tippet, and I probably had another one at the point where the line failed. I could have landed that bass if I had been meticulous enough about my tackle. In fact, I had the

The author seldom uses a net for bass. Here he is landing a largemouth by grasping its lower jaw between thumb and forefinger.

previous day landed a 7-pounder with the same test tippet—and this fish had another angler's 5/0 worm hook stuck in the corner of its mouth and trailed about 2 feet of 17- or 20-pound monofilament!

I've done some talking in this chapter, and elsewhere in this book, about 7- and 8-pound bass that I've taken on a fly rod. A lot of people don't quite believe this, but the truth is that even 9-pounders taken on a fly aren't too uncommon in lunker country. Just a few days ago, I was reading a newspaper article about a retired gentleman named Joe Pavesich who has an impressive record. During the past 5 years, he has placed among the top in the annual *Field & Stream* contest for largemouth bass caught on a fly rod. He won it once and placed second twice. In 1974, the 73-year-old angler came in second with a 9¼-pounder! His records indicate that since his retirement his fly rod has taken over 800 bass that weighed between 5 and 12¼ pounds!

The largest bass that I've caught to date on a fly rod weighed a little over 8 pounds. It hit a bug that I felt was large enough to interest bass but small enough to hook large bluegills. I was fishing along the edge of a grass bed in Florida's Lake Weir, picking up some bull bluegills and an occasional bass, when I found myself hemmed in by two other bass boats. One angler was fishing in a red boat behind me, maybe figuring that I wasn't hurting the bass population with my fly rod. The other boat, with two anglers aboard, was coming toward me. Something had to give, and I sort of treaded water with the electric motor while waiting to see what the oncoming boat was going to do. I was just off a good pocket in the grass, in which I had had a nice strike. While waiting, I made about a dozen casts into the pocket, working the bug very slowly. Off to the right, I noticed the weeds moving. I made a couple of more casts and, suddenly, some tiny minnows in the pocket started breaking water. Next cast, I aimed high so that my bug would settle gently, and the bass grabbed it almost before it got wet. The other boats were pretty close by now, and the anglers of course saw my rod bending.

The bass made a run toward the grass on the right side of the pocket, but fortunately I turned it, putting on as much pressure as I thought my tippet would take. Immediately I hit the start button on the foot-controlled pedal and nosed the boat away from the grass. I had my fish where I wanted it, and we fought it out in open water.

When it jumped, however, I suspected that it was hooked deep, and I was afraid that its "teeth" would abrade my tippet.

"Jeeze, what a bass!" said one of the guys in the boat in front of me.

"That's what it's all about," said the guy behind me in the red bass boat.

"Got a net?" said the third one.

The bass jumped again, closer in now. It had practically swallowed my bug.

"Jeeze, what a bass!"

"That's what it's all about."

"Do you need a net? I'll net it for you."

Well, I knew what it was all about and I wanted the other boats to lay off, and I certainly didn't want anybody swatting at my bass with a landing net under any circumstances and certainly not from another boat. Anyhow, the bass went around the boat a couple of times before it tired out. Cautiously, I brought it on in and gripped its lower jaw. Then I stood up in the boat and showed my fish.

"Jeeze, what a bass!"

"I'd a netted that fish."

"That's what it's all about," said the guy in the red boat. "I need me a fly rod."

The next afternoon, shortly before sundown, I thought maybe I ought to try the same grass bank again. When I headed the boat around the point, however, I saw that someone was fishing the pocket. He had anchored his red boat out a ways and was whipping a brand-new fly rod around, seeming to have difficulty in getting the bug out, much less into the pocket. Recognizing me, he redoubled his efforts.

This fellow seemed quite serious about his fishing, so I headed my boat on up the grass bank without telling him that he wasn't doing what it was all about. His quickness to try a fly rod, however, together with the success I had been having with popping bugs and flies, is what got me to thinking about writing this book. Fly-rodding for bass has increased tremendously during the past year and the trend is likely to continue. I think that a lot of the newcomers need a book on the subject, and I can only hope that this one helps them learn for themselves what it's all about.

Appendix

Fly-rodder's Guide
to
Gear and Tackle
Sources

NOTE: This annotated directory lists only manufacturers and mail-order sources of gear and tackle directly related to fly-fishing. A much longer listing of manufacturers of bass boats, electronic fishing aids, baitcasting gear, etc., was published in my book *Advanced Bass Tackle and Boats*.

Abercrombie & Fitch Company, P.O. Box 4288, Grand Central Station, New York, New York 10017. Fine things for anglers and other outdoorsmen. Seasonal catalogs are available, but some of these list only a limited amount of fishing gear. The best bet is to visit their store when you are in New York, San Francisco, Chicago, Palm Beach, and other cities. Take some money, though.

Aladdin Laboratories, Inc., 620 South 8th Street, Minneapolis, Minnesota 55404. Perrin automatic reels and aluminum fly boxes.

American Anglers, P.O. Box 521, Bethlehem, Pennsylvania 18016. Flies, tackle, and gear. Fly-tying tools and materials.

Angler's Den, Inc., P.O. Box 701, Linden, New Jersey 07036. Flies, fly-tying materials, lines, and miscellaneous gear. Fly rods and reels. Angler's Den is probably America's largest dealer in new and used bamboo rods.

Angler's Mail, 6497 Pearl Road, Cleveland, Ohio 44130. Rods, reels, fly lines, leaders, and other gear. Mail-order catalog available.

Anglers' Nook, P.O. Box 67A, Shushan, New York 12873. Flies, rods, reels, and gear. Fly-tying materials and tools.

Anglers Pro Shop, P.O. Box 35, Springfield, Ohio 45501. Rods, reels, flies, and gear. Rod-building materials.

Fred Arbogast Company, Inc., 313 West North Street, Akron, Ohio 44303. Arbogast makes several bass bugs. Their Hula Poppers feature rubber skirts, and they also market skirts that can be used on other bugs. Their Fin and Prescott divisions offer spinners, Wooly Worms, and other items of interest to fly-rodders.

Ashaway Line & Twine Manufacturing Company, Ashaway, Rhode Island 02804. Fly lines and backing line. Ashaway introduced the first dacron line in 1952.

Dan Bailey Flies and Tackle, P.O. Box 1019, Livingston, Montana 59047. Bailey's offers a large selection of flies, hair bugs, and streamers. Although they are based in trout country, the firm carries a number of saltwater flies as well as bass-size muddlers and streamers. Bailey's also markets rods, reels, waders, and miscellaneous fly-fishing gear and tackle, together with a large selection of fishing books. Catalog available; mail orders welcome.

Bassmaster Pro Shop, P.O. Box 3044, Montgomery, Alabama 36109. Operated by B.A.S.S., this mail-order source has recently introduced some fly-fishing gear to their line.

Bass Pro Shops, P.O. Box 441, Springfield, Missouri 65804. This large retail and mail-order house offers a complete line of baitcasting and spinning gear, as well as other gear and tackle for bassmen. They offer a few fly rods and reels, but the emphasis is on gear for hardware slingers.

Eddie Bauer, 1737 Airport Way South, Seattle, Washington 98134. This large mail-order house markets chic attire and gear for outdoorsmen. They have their own line of rods and reels. Custom-tied flies are available, and they offer a good selection of cork and hair bass bugs.

L. L. Bean, Inc., Freeport, Maine 04032. This delightful firm markets a good line of attire and gear for outdoorsmen. Their bass fishing line is rather limited, but they do carry such top-quality products as the Fenwick H.M.G. fly rods. Seasonal catalogs available.

Berkley and Company, Highways 9 and 71, Spirit Lake, Iowa 51360. Fly rods, reels, lines, and leaders.

Best Tackle Manufacturing Company, 3106 Bay Street, Unionville, Michigan 48767. Stanley Streamer swimming flies.

Betts Tackle Ltd., P.O. Box 57, Fuquay-Varina, North Carolina 27526. Flies, bugs, and other lures.

Bloss Flies, 137 Maple Hill Road, Blossburg, Pennsylvania 16912. Flies by C. Merton Pierce. Deer-hair bass bugs, including the Mississippi bass bugs, Henshall bugs, and the Bloss Bubble Pup. Fly-tying tools and materials. Mail-order catalog available.

Bodmer's Fly Shop, Inc., 2400 Naegele Road, Colorado Springs, Colorado 80904. Flies and fly-tying gear. Miscellaneous gear and tackle for fly-rodders. Catalog available.

Boone Bait Company, Inc., P.O. Box 571, Winter Park, Florida 32789. Popping bugs. Boone's Bee is probably the most popular bug in the state of Florida.

Browning, Route 1, Morgan, Utah 84050. Fly rods and reels.

Gene Bullard Custom Rods, 10139 Shoreview Road, Dallas, Texas 75238. Custom rods; graphite blanks and other rod-building materials. Mail-order catalog available.

Burke Fishing Lures, 1969 South Airport Road, Traverse City, Michigan 49684. Soft plastic lures and critters.

California Tackle Company, Inc., 430 West Redondo Beach Boulevard, Gardena, California 90284. Sabre rods. Rod blanks and hardware.

Cape Cod Line Company, Division of Brownell & Company, Inc., Moodus, Connecticut 06469. Lines.

Cascade Tackle Company, 2425 Diamond Lake Boulevard, Rosebury, Oregon 97470. Rods, reels, flies, fly-tying materials, and miscellaneous gear.

Lew Childre & Son, Inc., P.O. Box 535, Foley, Alabama 36535. Fly rods and Fuji aluminum oxide rod guides.

Dale Clemens Custom Tackle, Route 3, Box 415, Allentown, Pennsylvania 18104. Custom rods and rod-building materials.

Columbia Company, P.O. Box G, Columbia, Alabama 36319. Lures and bugs.

Dave Cook Sporting Goods Company, 16th and Market Streets, Denver, Colorado 80201. Rods, reels, lines, flies, and miscellaneous gear. Mail-order catalog available.

Coren's Rod & Reel Service, 6619 North Clark Street, Chicago, Illinois 60626. Rod-building materials.

Cortland Line Company, P.O. Box 1362, Cortland, New York 13045. Micro-Foam fly lines and Micron backing line. Other fly lines and leaders. Rods, reels, and fishing vests for fly-rodders.

Creme Lure Company, P.O. Box 87, Tyler, Texas 75701. Soft plastic lures. Lots of 'em.

J. Lee Cuddy Associates, 450 N.E. 79th Street, Miami, Florida 33138. Blanks and rod-building materials. Other items for anglers.

Daiwa, 14011 South Normandie Avenue, Gardena, California 90249. Daiwa offers a limited line of fly reels and rods.

DeLong Lures, Inc., 85 Compark Road, Centerville, Ohio 45459. Soft plastic lures.

Jack Dickerson's, Lake of the Ozarks, Camdenton, Missouri 65020. Tackle and gear for outdoorsmen. Fly rods, reels, bugs, etc. Catalog available.

Dragon Fly Company, P.O. Drawer 1349, Sumter, South Carolina 29150. Flies, bugs, and lures.

Falls Bait Company, Inc., 1440 Kennedy Road, Chippewa Falls, Wisconsin 54729. Poppers and other bugs.

Featherweight Products, 3545–58 Ocean View Boulevard, Glendale, California 91208. Rawhide rod blanks; rod-building hardware, tools, and materials.

Fenwick, P.O. Box 729, Westminster, California 92683. Fiberglass and graphite rods.

Feurer Brothers, Inc., 77 Lafayette Avenue, North White Plains, New York 10603. Reels.

Finnysports, 2910 Glanzman Road, Toledo, Ohio 43614. Gear and materials for fly tiers, lure makers, and rod builders. Miscellaneous fishing tackle. Catalog available.

Fireside Angler, Inc., P.O. Box 823, Melville, New York 11746. Fly-tying tools and materials. Rods, reels, flies, and gear. Books. Catalog available.

The Fly and Tackle Shop, P.O. Box 172, Bluff City, Tennessee 37618. Custom flies and deer-hair bugs.

The Fly Fisherman's Bookcase and Tackle Service, Route 9A, Croton-on-Hudson, New York 10520. This firm carries a large stock of flies and lures (including bass bugs), as well as rods, reels, waders, and so on. Fly-tying tools and materials. Books. Write for a catalog.

The Gaines Company, P.O. Box 35, Gaines, Pennsylvania 16921. Cork popping bugs.

Bill Gallasch Flies, 8705 Weldon Drive, Richmond, Virginia 23229. Custom-made bugs, flies, and streamers.

Gapen Tackle Company, Highway 10, Big Lake, Minnesota 55309. Muddler Minnows and other flies and lures.

Garcia Corporation, 329 Alfred Avenue, Teaneck, New Jersey 07666. Fly rods, reels, and lines.

Gene's Tackle Shop, P.O. Box 7701, Rochester, New York 14622. Fly-tying tools and materials.

Gladding-South Bend Tackle Company, Inc., South Otselic, New York 13155. Fly rods, reels, lines, fishing vests, etc. Gladding's Glen L. Evans division (Caldwell, Idaho) offers flies, streamers, and bugs.

Ted Godfrey's Custom Flies, 9428 Rose Hill Drive, Bethesda, Maryland 20034. Flies and hair bugs. Godfrey's ties a flat hair bug that casts better than anything I've seen of comparable size; because it is flat on top and bottom, it has a low wind resistance. Catalog available.

Grassl's Double OO, River Falls, Wisconsin 54022. Flies, bugs, and miscellaneous gear.

Gudebrod Brothers Silk Company, Inc., 12 South 12th Street, Philadelphia, Pennsylvania 19107. Fly lines and dacron backing line. Rod-making materials.

Hackle & Tackle Company, 553 North Salina Street, Syracuse, New York 13208. Fly-tying tools and materials; rods, reels, lines, and gear. Books. Mail-order catalog available.

The Hackle House, 4117 Peralta Boulevard, Fremont, California 94536. Fly-tying materials.

Harrington & Richardson, Inc., Industrial Row, Gardner, Massachusetts 01440. Distributors of the Hardy line of British-made fly rods, reels, lines, and gear. Catalog available.

James Heddon's Sons, 414 West Street, Dowagiac, Michigan 49047. Fly rods and reels.

Herter's, Route 1, Waseca, Minnesota 56903. Everything. Send for one of their huge catalogs.

John J. Hildebrandt Corporation, P.O. Box 50, Logansport, Indiana 46947. Spinner blades, jig spinners, a few flies, and plastic skirts.

E. Hille, P.O. Box 269, Williamsport, Pennsylvania 17701. Tools and materials for fly tying and rod making. Tackle boxes, fishing tubes, and so on. Catalog available.

International Hook and Tackle, 1830 South Acoma Street, Denver, Colorado 80223. Hooks. Miscellaneous hardware for tackle makers.

Joe's Tackle Shop, 186 Main Street, Warehouse Point, Connecticut 06088. Rods, reels, fly-tying equipment. Miscellaneous tackle. Price list available.

Poul Jorgensen's Artistic Fishing Flies, 604 Providence Road, Towson, Maryland 21204. Custom flies.

The Keel Fly Company, P.O. Box 8499, Toledo, Ohio 43623. This firm markets a number of streamers and flies tied on keel hooks, including the Keel Miracle Bug, a sort of weedless fly bug dressed with deer hair. They also market a few other items of interest to fly-rodders.

H. L. Leonard Rod Company, 25 Cottage Street, Midland Park, New Jersey 07432. Bamboo, fiberglass, and graphite rods. Fly reels, lines, leaders, etc. Miscellaneous gear. Large selection of flies, streamers, and bugs. Outdoor attire. Catalog available.

Bud Lilly's, P.O. Box 387, West Yellowstone, Montana 59758. Flies and fly-fishing gear. Fly-tying tools and materials. Catalog available.

Marathon Tackle, Route 2, Mosinee, Wisconsin 54455. Bass bugs, streamers, and flies.

Martin Reel Company, Inc., P.O. Drawer 8, Mohawk, New York 13407. Wide selection of fly rods and reels. Martin made the first automatic fly reel back in 1884. They also market flies, streamers, and lines.

Mason Tackle Company, Otisville, Michigan 48463. Lines and leaders.

Midland Tackle Company, 66 Route 17, Sloatsburg, New York 10974.

Miscellaneous fishing gear. Tools and materials for fly tiers, lure makers, and rod builders.

O. Mustad & Son, Inc., P.O. Box 838, Auburn, New York 13021. Hooks since 1832. Anyone interested in hooks should ask for a copy of their catalog.

Netcraft Company, 3101 Sylvania Street, Toledo, Ohio 43613. Rods, reels, lines, lures, bugs, etc. Tools and materials for do-it-yourselfers. Catalog available.

Newton Line Company, Inc., Homer, New York 13077. Lines.

Ojai Fisherman, 218 North Encinal Avenue, Ojai, California 93023. Fly-tying tools and materials. Flies, rods, books, and miscellaneous gear. Catalog available.

OLM International Corporation, 145 Sylvester Road, South San Francisco, California 94080. Fly reels, waders, and other gear.

The Orvis Company, Inc., Manchester, Vermont 05254. Fine bamboo, graphite, and fiberglass rods. Good selection of fly reels, lines, and so forth. Flies and bugs. Attire and miscellaneous gear for outdoorsmen. Catalog available.

E. H. Peckinpaugh Company, P.O. Box 15044, Baton Rouge, Louisiana 70815. Bass bugs.

Pflueger Sporting Goods Division, P.O. Box 310, Hallandale, Florida 33009. Medalist fly reels, rods, and lines. Their Mono-Fly line has an inner core of extruded monofilament; their construction technique permits them to make a 105-foot line consisting of continuous shooting head and shooting line. Neat.

Phillips Fly & Tackle Company, P.O. Box 188, Alexandria, Pennsylvania 16611. Flies, streamers, and bass bugs.

Phillipson Fishing Rods, 3M Company, 3M Center, St. Paul, Minnesota 55101. Phillipson Scotchply fly rods.

Powell Rod Company, 1148 West 8th Avenue, Chico, California 95926. Custom-made rods; fiberglass and bamboo models, from $50 to $400.

Rangeley Region Sports Shop, 28 Main Street, Rangeley, Maine 04970. Rods, reels, lines, and miscellaneous gear for fly-fishing. Flies and fly-tying materials. Books. Catalog available.

Reed Tackle, P.O. Box 390, Caldwell, New Jersey 07066. Fly-tying materials and tools. Cork bug bodies, spinners, hooks, etc. Rod blanks and fittings. Catalog available.

Hank Roberts Outfitters, P.O. Box 308, Boulder, Colorado 80302. Flies, rods, reels, lines, etc. Fly-tying tools and materials. According to their catalog, their 1/0 hair mouse is a great bass catcher, and even fooled their cat. Their large fly selection includes weighted Wooly Worms and large keel patterns.

Rod and Reel, P.O. Box 132, Leola, Pennsylvania 17540. Rods, reels, and gear. Custom flies. Fly-tying tools and materials. Catalog available.

Raymond C. Rumpf & Son, P.O. Box 176, Ferndale, Pennsylvania 18921. Fly-tying materials and tools. Hair bass bugs, flies, and streamers. Catalog available.

St. Croix Corporation, 9909 South Shore Drive, Minneapolis, Minnesota 55441. Fly rods and reels.

Scientific Anglers, Inc., P.O. Box 2001, Midland, Michigan 48640. System-balanced fly-fishing gear, including rods, reels, and the Air Cel lines. Their reels are made by Hardy Brothers in England.

Sears Roebuck and Company, Sears Tower, Chicago, Illinois 60684. Rods, reels, lines, and miscellaneous gear. Write for their Boating and Fishing Catalog.

Shakespeare, 241 East Kalamazoo Avenue, Kalamazoo, Michigan 49001. Fly rods, reels, lines. Shakespeare also manufactures a large line of baitcasting, spinning, and electronic gear for bass anglers.

Spin-Line, 16 Thomas Street, Kingston, New York 12401. Flies and miscellaneous gear. Catalog available.

Sports Liquidators, P.O. Box E, Sun Valley, California 91352. Discounted gear.

J. M. Stott, P.O. Box 971, Kissimmee, Florida 32741. Flies and bugs. Several poppers and hair bugs, as well as large bass-size streamers.

Streamborn Flies, 13055 S.W. Pacific Highway, Tigard, Oregon 97223. Flies and fly-fishing gear. Fly-tying tools and materials. Books. Rod-building materials. Catalog available.

Streamside Anglers, P.O. Box 2158, Missoula, Montana 59801. Hand-tied flies, rods, reels, lines, etc. Fly-tying tools and materials. Books. Informative catalog available.

Sunrise Sports Center, P.O. Box 2003, Rochester, New Hampshire 03867. Flies.

Sunset Line & Twine Company, Jefferson and Erwin Streets, Petaluma, California 94952. This firm makes miscellaneous fishing lines, and they are the United States distributor for Masterline British-made fly lines.

Tackle-Craft, P.O. Box 280, Chippewa Falls, Wisconsin 54729. Tools and materials for making flies, bugs, and lures. Rods, reels, and lines. Catalog available.

Tack-L-Tyers, 939 Chicago Avenue, Evanston, Illinois 60202. Fly- and bug-tying kits, materials, and tools.

Thomas & Thomas Company, 4 Fiske Avenue, Greenfield, Massachusetts 01301. Fine bamboo rods.

D. H. Thompson, 335 Walnut Avenue, Elgin, Illinois 60120. Fly-tying tools.

Norm Thompson, 1805 N.W. Thurman Street, Portland, Oregon 97209. Flies, bugs, and fine tackle. Interesting gear and attire for all anglers. Catalog available.

Uncle Josh Bait Company, 524 Clarence Street, Fort Atkinson, Wisconsin 53538. Pork rind and lures.

Universal Imports, P.O. Box 1581, Ann Arbor, Michigan 48106. Fly-tying materials.

U.S. Line Company, Inc., 22 Main Street, Westfield, Massachusetts 01085. Fly lines, backing lines, tackle boxes, and other gear.

Uslan Rods, 18679 West Dixie Highway, North Miami Beach, Florida 33160. Custom-made bamboo rods, featuring five-strip construction. Available in lengths of 7 to 9 feet, at $150 to $200.

Val-Craft, Inc., 67 North Worcester Street, Chartley, Massachusetts 02712. Valentine fly reels with planetary gearing.

Weber Tackle Company, Stevens Point, Wisconsin 54481. Flies, bass bugs, streamers, tapered leaders, and miscellaneous gear.

R. L. Winston Rod Company, 475 Third Street, San Francisco, California 94107. Fine bamboo and fiberglass rods. Winston also offers a repair service for split-bamboo rods.

Woodland Fly Shop, Route 30, Adirondack Trail, Mayfield, New York 12117. Flies.

Woodstream Corporation, P.O. Box 327, Lititz, Pennsylvania 17543. Fly rods and reels. Old Pal tackle boxes and gear.

Wright & McGill Company, 4245 East 46th Avenue, Denver, Colorado 80216. Eagle Claw hooks. Fly rods and reels.

Paul H. Young Company, 14039 Peninsula Drive, Traverse City, Michigan 49684. Custom-built bamboo fly rods.

Index